Mastering Dart Programming: Modern Web Development

Kameron Hussain and Frahaan Hussain

Published by Sonar Publishing, 2024.

MASTERING DART PROGRAMMING: MODERN WEB DEVELOPMENT

First edition. January 25, 2024.

ISBN: 979-8224866175

Written by Kameron Hussain and Frahaan Hussain.

Table of Contents

Chapter 1: Introduction to Dart

1.1 The Evolution of Dart: History and Purpose

1.2 Setting Up Your Dart Environment

Installing Dart SDK

Verifying the Installation

Using DartPad

Integrated Development Environments (IDEs)

Creating Your First Dart Project

1.3 Understanding the Syntax: A First Look

Hello, Dart!

Variables and Data Types

Comments

Operators

Control Structures

Conclusion

1.4 Dart and the Web: Why It Matters

Performance

Developer Productivity

Code Reusability

Web Components and Libraries

Strongly Typed Language

Frameworks and Tools

Growing Community

1.5 The Dart Community: Resources and Support

Official Documentation

Dart Pub

Dart GitHub Repository

Dart Dev Community

Stack Overflow

Dart Gitter Chat

Conferences and Meetups

Dart Blog and Twitter

Online Tutorials and Courses

Local User Groups

Chapter 2: Basic Concepts in Dart

2.1 Variables and Data Types

Declaring Variables

Dynamic Type

Constants

String Interpolation

Type Conversions

Null Safety

2.2 Control Flow: Making Decisions in Dart

Conditional Statements

Switch Statements

Loops

Breaking and Continuing Loops

2.3 Functions and Methods: Basics

Defining Functions

Function Parameters

Return Values

Optional Parameters

Anonymous Functions (Closures)

Method

2.4 Collections: Lists, Maps, and Sets

Lists

Maps

Sets

2.5 Error Handling and Exceptions

Exceptions in Dart

Throwing Exceptions

Catching Exceptions

Finally Block

Rethrowing Exceptions

Custom Exceptions

Chapter 3: Advanced Dart Programming

3.1 Object-Oriented Programming in Dart

Classes and Objects

Encapsulation

Inheritance

Polymorphism

Abstraction and Interfaces

Getters and Setters

3.2 Understanding Async Programming and Futures

Asynchronous vs. Synchronous Code

Futures in Dart

async and await

Error Handling with Futures

Concurrent Asynchronous Operations

3.3 Advanced Collections and Iterables

Advanced Collections

Iterable Operations

3.4 Generics: Types and Collections

Introduction to Generics

Generic Functions

Generic Collections

3.5 Effective Dart: Best Practices

Code Formatting

Effective Use of Linter Rules

Effective Use of Asynchronous Code

Effective Use of Comments

Effective Use of Named Constructors

Chapter 4: Dart and Web Development

4.1 Introduction to Web Programming with Dart

Dart for Web Development

Building Web Apps with Dart

The Dart SDK for the Web

Transpiling to JavaScript

4.2 Dart and HTML: A Seamless Interaction

Dart and the DOM

Event Handling

Data Binding

HTML Templates

4.3 Managing Web APIs and HTTP Requests

The dart:html Library

The http Package

Handling CORS

Authentication

Error Handling

4.4 Building Interactive Web Applications

Event Handling and DOM Manipulation

Client-Side Routing

Web Components

State Management

4.5 Dart in the World of Web Frameworks

AngularDart

Flutter for Web

Shelf

Aqueduct

Chapter 5: Mobile App Development with Flutter

5.1 Flutter: The Future of Mobile Development

Fast Development with Hot Reload

Single Codebase, Multiple Platforms

Rich Set of Customizable Widgets

High Performance

Strong Community and Ecosystem

5.2 Setting Up a Flutter Environment

Prerequisites

Installing Flutter

Installing Dart

Configuring Your IDE

Android and iOS Setup

5.3 Basics of Flutter Development with Dart

Creating Your First Flutter App

Understanding Flutter Widgets

Stateful Widgets and Interactivity

Flutter's Rich Ecosystem

5.4 Designing User Interfaces in Flutter

Flutter's Widget System

Building a Basic UI

Styling and Theming

Layouts and Widgets

Responsive UI Design

5.5 State Management in Flutter Apps

What is State in Flutter?

Local State Management

Global State Management

Chapter 6: Dart and Databases

6.1 Introduction to Databases in Dart

6.2 Working with SQL Databases

SQLite in Dart

Performing Database Operations

Error Handling and Transactions

6.3 NoSQL Databases: An Overview

What Are NoSQL Databases?

NoSQL Databases in Dart

Cloud-Based NoSQL Solutions

6.4 Dart and Firebase: Real-Time Data Handling

Firebase Realtime Database

Firebase Firestore

Choosing Between Firebase Realtime Database and Firestore

6.5 Effective Data Persistence Strategies

Local Storage

SQLite Databases

Cloud-Based Solutions

7.1 Writing Testable Code in Dart

The Importance of Testable Code

1. Quality Assurance

2. Code Confidence

3. Collaboration

4. Maintainability

Writing Testable Dart Code

1. Separation of Concerns

2. Dependency Injection

3. Mocking and Stubbing

4. Immutability

5. Test-Driven Development (TDD)

6. Code Coverage

7. Continuous Integration

8. Use Testing Frameworks

Conclusion

7.2 Unit Testing and Integration Testing

Unit Testing

Integration Testing

Test Driven Development (TDD)

Continuous Integration (CI)

7.3 Debugging Techniques in Dart

1. Print Statements

2. Debugger in IDEs

3. Logging

4. Dart DevTools

5. Remote Debugging

6. Exception Handling

7. Testing and Test-Driven Development (TDD)

7.4 Performance Tuning and Optimization

1. Profiling Your Code

2. Reduce Redundant Operations

3. Use Efficient Data Structures

4. Avoid Unnecessary Render Operations in Flutter

5. Optimize Network Requests

6. Memory Management

7. Testing and Profiling

8. Lazy Loading

7.5 Continuous Integration and Delivery in Dart

1. Continuous Integration (CI)

2. Continuous Delivery (CD)

3. Monitoring and Rollback

8.1 Standard Libraries in Dart

1. dart:core

2. dart:io

3. dart:html

4. dart:convert

8.2 Third-Party Packages: Integration and Usage

Installing Packages with pub

Importing and Using Packages

Example: Using the http Package

Version Constraints

Package Documentation

8.3 Creating and Publishing Your Own Dart Package

Creating a Dart Package

Publishing Your Package

Maintaining Your Package

8.4 Package Management with Pub

Understanding pubspec.yaml

Installing Dependencies

Upgrading Dependencies

Managing Dev Dependencies

Lock Files

Publishing Your Own Packages

8.5 Keeping Your Code Updated and Secure

Regularly Update Dependencies

Security Audits and Vulnerability Scanning

Code Reviews and Static Analysis

Stay Informed About Security Updates

Continuous Integration and Automated Testing

Conclusion

Chapter 9: Interfacing with Other Languages

9.1 Dart and JavaScript: Bridging the Gap

The JavaScript Interop Library

Importing JavaScript Code

Calling JavaScript Functions

Accessing JavaScript Objects

JavaScript Promises and Futures

Interoperability Caveats

Conclusion

9.2 Calling C and C++ Code from Dart

Dart FFI (Foreign Function Interface)

Creating a Dart FFI Library

Handling Data Types

Memory Management

Error Handling

Conclusion

9.3 Dart FFI (Foreign Function Interface)

Using Dart FFI

Data Types and Conversions

Memory Management

Error Handling

Conclusion

9.4 Mobile Platform Integration: Android and iOS

Flutter for Cross-Platform Development

Platform Channels

Platform-Specific Implementations

Conclusion

9.5 Exploring Other Language Interoperability

Using Dart FFI

Interoperability with Other Languages

Conclusion

Chapter 10: Advanced UI with Flutter

10.1 Advanced Widgets and Layouts in Flutter

Introduction to Advanced Widgets

Advanced Layouts

Responsive Design

Conclusion

10.2 Custom Animation and Motion Design

Animation Basics

Using Animated Widgets

Creating Custom Animations

Motion Design and Physics

Conclusion

10.3 Integrating Multimedia Elements

Displaying Images

Adding Icons

Audio Playback

Video Playback

Camera and Augmented Reality (AR)

Conclusion

10.4 Responsive and Adaptive Design Principles

Understanding Responsiveness

Adaptive Layouts

Handling Orientation Changes

Conclusion

10.5 Flutter for Desktop and Web Applications

Desktop Support with Flutter

Web Support with Flutter

Conclusion

Chapter 11: State Management in Dart

Section 11.1: Understanding State Management

The Significance of State

State in Dart Applications

Challenges of State Management

State Management Techniques

Selecting the Right State Management Approach

Section 11.2: Global State vs Local State

Global State

Local State

Choosing Between Global and Local State

Section 11.3: Popular State Management Techniques

1. setState()

2. InheritedWidget

3. Provider

4. Bloc Pattern (with Flutter Bloc)

5. GetX

Section 11.4: Streams and RxDart for Reactive Programming

Understanding Streams

Introducing RxDart

Using RxDart in Flutter

Section 11.5: Best Practices in State Management

1. Use Provider or Riverpod for Small to Medium-Sized Apps

2. Employ Bloc for Complex Logic

3. Organize State into Models and Services

4. Minimize the Use of Global State

5. Leverage Immutable Data

6. Optimize Rebuilds with const Widgets

7. Debounce User Input for Search and Filtering

8. Implement State Restoration

9. Profile and Optimize Performance

10. Stay Updated with Best Practices

Chapter 12: Asynchronous Programming in Dart

Section 12.1: The Role of Asynchrony in Modern Development

Understanding Blocking vs. Non-blocking Code

Use Cases for Asynchronous Programming

Dart's Asynchronous Model

Section 12.2: Working with Futures and Streams

Futures

Streams

Combining Futures and Streams

Section 12.3: Advanced Async Patterns and Techniques

Future Combinators

Streams Transformation

Section 12.4: Error Handling in Asynchronous Code

Handling Errors in Futures

Handling Errors in Streams

Section 12.5: Practical Applications of Asynchronous Programming

1. Fetching Data from External Sources

2. Parallel Processing

3. Timed Operations

4. Reactive Programming

5. Concurrent I/O Operations

Chapter 13: Design Patterns and Architecture

Section 13.1: Introduction to Design Patterns in Dart

What Are Design Patterns?

Benefits of Using Design Patterns

Applying Design Patterns in Dart

Section 13.2: Structural, Creational, and Behavioral Patterns

Creational Patterns

Structural Patterns

Behavioral Patterns

Section 13.3: Implementing MVC and MVVM in Dart

Model-View-Controller (MVC)

Model-View-ViewModel (MVVM)

Section 13.4: Dependency Injection and Inversion of Control

Understanding Dependency Injection (DI)

Exploring Inversion of Control (IoC)

Practical Benefits of DI and IoC

Using DI and IoC in Dart

Section 13.5: Building Scalable Application Architecture

Why Scalability Matters

Architectural Principles for Scalability

Dart and Scalability

Chapter 14: Network Programming in Dart

Section 14.1: Basics of Network Communication

Understanding Network Communication

Dart's Network Libraries

Making HTTP Requests

WebSocket Communication

Section 14.2: HTTP and Web Sockets in Dart

HTTP Communication

WebSocket Communication

Section 14.3: Creating RESTful APIs with Dart

What is RESTful API?

Creating RESTful APIs with Dart

Conclusion

Section 14.4: Authentication and Authorization Strategies

Authentication vs. Authorization

Implementing Authentication

Implementing Authorization

Conclusion

Section 14.5: Best Practices in Network Security

1. Use HTTPS (TLS/SSL)

2. Input Validation

3. Authentication Tokens

4. Authorization

5. Rate Limiting

6. Content Security Policy (CSP)

7. Cross-Origin Resource Sharing (CORS)

8. Error Handling

9. Regular Security Audits

10. Security Headers

Chapter 15: Graphics and Animation in Dart

Section 15.1: Drawing Basics with Canvas

Section 15.2: Creating Custom Graphics and Shapes

Basic Drawing Operations

Advanced Custom Graphics

Section 15.3: Animation Principles in Dart

The Animation Loop

Easing Functions

Frame Rate and Performance

Section 15.4: Interactive Graphics and User Interfaces

Event Handling

Canvas Graphics

User Interface Libraries

Responsiveness and Layout

Section 15.5: Integrating 3D Graphics with WebGL

What is WebGL?

Using WebGL with Dart

Creating 3D Scenes

WebGL Considerations

Chapter 16: Dart for IoT and Embedded Systems

Section 16.1: Introduction to IoT with Dart

Section 16.2: Dart on Embedded Systems

Section 16.3: Building IoT Applications with Dart

Section 16.4: Communication Protocols and Hardware Integration

Section 16.5: Case Studies: Dart in IoT Projects

Chapter 16: Dart for IoT and Embedded Systems

Section 16.1: Introduction to IoT with Dart

IoT Fundamentals

Dart's Role in IoT

Challenges and Opportunities

Section 16.2: Dart on Embedded Systems

Dart on Embedded Platforms

Advantages of Using Dart on Embedded Systems

Use Cases for Dart in Embedded Systems

Dart's Limitations in Embedded Systems

Section 16.3: Building IoT Applications with Dart

Key Components of IoT Applications

Developing IoT Applications with Dart

Example IoT Use Cases with Dart

Challenges and Considerations

Section 16.4: Communication Protocols and Hardware Integration

Communication Protocols

Hardware Integration

Example: MQTT Communication with Dart

Section 16.5: Case Studies: Dart in IoT Projects

Case Study 1: Smart Home Automation

Case Study 2: Industrial Monitoring and Control

Case Study 3: Environmental Monitoring

Case Study 4: Agriculture and Precision Farming

Chapter 17: Dart for Server-Side Development

Section 17.1: Setting Up a Dart Server

Section 17.2: Building Web Servers and APIs

Creating a Simple Web Server

Routing and Handling Multiple Endpoints

Building RESTful APIs

Section 17.3: Working with Middleware in Dart

Adding Middleware to Your Dart Server

Creating Custom Middleware

Middleware for Authentication and Authorization

Section 17.4: Scalability and Performance Optimization

1. Asynchronous Programming

2. Connection Pooling

3. Caching

4. Load Balancing

5. Profiling and Monitoring

6. Proper Error Handling

7. Caching Responses

Section 17.5: Case Studies: Dart in Server-Side Applications

1. Aqueduct Framework for RESTful APIs

2. Shelf: A Lightweight Middleware Framework

3. Fuchsia Operating System

4. Firebase Functions for Serverless Computing

5. Angel Framework for Full-Stack Development

Chapter 18: Dart and Machine Learning

Section 18.1: Introduction to Machine Learning in Dart

The Role of Machine Learning

Dart and Machine Learning

Section 18.2: Data Processing and Analysis

Data Preprocessing

Exploratory Data Analysis (EDA)

Data Transformation

Conclusion

Section 18.3: Integrating Dart with ML Frameworks

TensorFlow and TFLite

MLKit

Dart Libraries for Machine Learning

Python Integration

Conclusion

Section 18.4: Building Predictive Models in Dart

Data Preparation

Supervised Learning

Unsupervised Learning

Evaluating Models

Deployment

Section 18.5: Real-World Applications of Dart in ML

1. Mobile App Development with ML

2. IoT and Edge Devices

3. Web-Based ML Applications

4. Custom ML Solutions

5. Integration with Other ML Ecosystems

Chapter 19: Game Development with Dart

Section 19.1: Introduction to Game Development in Dart

Why Choose Dart for Game Development?

Getting Started with Game Development in Dart

Creating Your First Dart Game

Section 19.2: Game Loops and Rendering Techniques

Understanding the Game Loop

Implementing a Game Loop in Dart

Efficient Rendering Techniques

Section 19.3: Physics and Collision Detection

Physics Simulations

Collision Detection

Section 19.4: Building 2D and 3D Games

2D Game Development

3D Game Development

Section 19.5: Publishing and Monetizing Dart Games

Choosing the Right Platforms

Publishing on App Stores

Monetization Strategies

Chapter 20: The Future of Dart

Section 20.1: Emerging Trends and Technologies

1. WebAssembly (Wasm) Integration

2. Quantum Computing

3. Dart for AI and Machine Learning

4. Extended Platform Support

5. Enhanced Web Frameworks

6. Cross-Platform Development Domination

7. Improved Tooling and IDE Support

8. Community and Collaborations

Section 20.2: Dart in the World of Quantum Computing

Quantum Computing Primer

Dart's Role in Quantum Computing

Quantum Computing Libraries and Frameworks

Preparing for the Quantum Future

Section 20.3: The Role of Dart in Large-Scale Systems

Scalability and Dart

Maintainability and Dart

Performance Optimization and Dart

Envisioning the Future

Section 20.4: Dart Community: Contributions and Collaborations

Open Source Development

Package Ecosystem

Dart Web and Flutter

Community Support and Education

Conclusion

Section 20.5: Envisioning the Next Decade of Dart Development

1. Language Evolution

2. Dart for Web Development

3. Dart and Flutter

4. Community and Collaboration

5. Emerging Technologies

6. Education and Adoption

7. Industry Adoption

Chapter 1: Introduction to Dart

1.1 The Evolution of Dart: History and Purpose

Dart is a programming language that was developed by Google. It was first unveiled to the public in 2011, with the goal of addressing the limitations of JavaScript for web development. At the time, JavaScript was the dominant language for building web applications, but it had its shortcomings, such as lack of type safety and performance issues. Dart aimed to provide a more modern and efficient alternative.

The development of Dart was driven by the need for a language that could be used for building large-scale web applications. Google was heavily invested in web technologies, and they saw the potential for a language that could make it easier to build complex and interactive web applications. Dart was designed with a focus on performance, scalability, and maintainability.

One of the key features of Dart is its optional static typing system. While JavaScript is dynamically typed, Dart allows developers to specify types for variables and function parameters. This provides better tooling support, as IDEs can offer features like code completion and type checking. At the same time, Dart remains flexible, allowing developers to choose when and where to use static typing.

Another important aspect of Dart is its ability to run both in web browsers and on server-side environments. This versatility allows developers to use Dart for full-stack development, creating web applications that share code between the client and server. This approach can lead to code reuse and improved consistency in web applications.

Dart's development has continued to evolve over the years. It has gained support for various platforms, including mobile app development through the Flutter framework. Google's investment in Dart has also led to its adoption in various projects and applications, solidifying its place in the world of programming languages.

In the next sections of this chapter, we will delve deeper into Dart, covering topics such as setting up your Dart environment, understanding the syntax, and exploring its significance in web development. Whether you are a newcomer to Dart or looking to expand your knowledge, this chapter will serve as a foundation for your journey into the world of Dart programming.

1.2 Setting Up Your Dart Environment

Setting up your development environment is the first step towards getting started with Dart programming. In this section, we'll walk you through the process of setting up your Dart development environment so that you can start writing and running Dart code.

Installing Dart SDK

The Dart Software Development Kit (SDK) is the core package you need to start working with Dart. To install it, follow these steps:

1. Visit the official Dart website at dart.dev[1].
2. Navigate to the "Get Started" section and choose the installation method that suits your operating system (Windows, macOS, or Linux).
3. Follow the installation instructions provided for your

1. https://dart.dev/

specific platform.

Once the installation is complete, you should have the Dart SDK installed on your system.

Verifying the Installation

To ensure that Dart is installed correctly, open your terminal or command prompt and run the following command:

dart—version

You should see the Dart version displayed in the output, confirming that Dart is successfully installed on your system.

Using DartPad

If you prefer a lightweight online development environment for trying out Dart code without installing anything locally, you can use DartPad[2]. DartPad allows you to write and run Dart code directly in your web browser, making it a great choice for quick experimentation.

Integrated Development Environments (IDEs)

To make your Dart development more efficient, you can use integrated development environments (IDEs) that offer Dart support. Some popular choices include:

- **Visual Studio Code (VS Code)**: VS Code is a popular, free, and open-source code editor that provides excellent support for Dart development. You can install the Dart extension from the VS Code marketplace to enhance your Dart coding experience.

2. https://dartpad.dev/

- **Android Studio**: If you're planning to develop mobile applications using Dart and Flutter, Android Studio is an IDE that offers robust Flutter and Dart support out of the box.

- **IntelliJ IDEA**: JetBrains' IntelliJ IDEA is a powerful IDE that also offers Dart support through plugins. If you're already familiar with IntelliJ IDEA, you can use it for Dart development as well.

Creating Your First Dart Project

Now that you have Dart installed and an IDE set up (if desired), you can create your first Dart project. You can start by opening your chosen IDE or a code editor and creating a new Dart project or simply creating a new Dart file with a .dart extension.

Here's a simple "Hello, World!" example in Dart:

```
void main() {

print("Hello, World!");

}
```

You can save this code in a .dart file and run it using the Dart SDK. The main() function is the entry point of your Dart program, and print() is used to output text to the console.

With your Dart environment set up and your first Dart program written, you're ready to start exploring the language further. In the following sections of this book, we'll dive deeper into Dart's syntax, features, and its role in web and mobile development.

1.3 Understanding the Syntax: A First Look

Dart's syntax is designed to be clean and readable, making it accessible to both beginners and experienced developers. In this section, we'll provide you with a first look at Dart's syntax and its fundamental elements.

Hello, Dart!

Let's start with a simple Dart program that prints "Hello, Dart!" to the console:

```
void main() {

print("Hello, Dart!");

}
```

- void main(): This is the entry point of a Dart program. It's where execution begins. In Dart, the main function is a special function that serves as the entry point.
- print("Hello, Dart!");: This line uses the print function to display "Hello, Dart!" in the console. In Dart, you use parentheses () to call functions, and strings are enclosed in double quotes ".

Variables and Data Types

Dart is a statically typed language, which means that variables have a specific data type that is known at compile time. Here are some common data types in Dart:

- int: Represents integer values, e.g., int age = 30;.

- double: Represents floating-point (decimal) values, e.g., double price = 19.99;.

- String: Represents sequences of characters, e.g., String name = "Alice";.

- bool: Represents boolean values (true or false), e.g., bool isDartFun = true;.

You can declare variables using the var keyword, which allows Dart to infer the data type based on the assigned value:

var age = 30; // Dart infers the type as int

var price = 19.99; // Dart infers the type as double

var name = "Alice"; // Dart infers the type as String

var isDartFun = true; // Dart infers the type as bool

Comments

In Dart, you can add comments to your code to provide explanations or documentation. Dart supports both single-line comments using // and multi-line comments using /* */:

// This is a single-line comment

/*

This is a

multi-line comment

*/

Operators

Dart provides various operators for performing operations on variables and values. Some common operators include:

- Arithmetic operators: +, -, *, /, % (remainder)
- Comparison operators: ==, !=, <, >, <=, >=
- Logical operators: && (and), || (or), ! (not)

Here's an example of using operators:

```
int a = 10;

int b = 5;

int sum = a + b; // Addition

int difference = a - b; // Subtraction

int product = a * b; // Multiplication

double quotient = a / b; // Division (result is a double)

int remainder = a % b; // Remainder

bool isEqual = (a == b); // Comparison

bool isTrue = true;

bool isFalse = !isTrue; // Logical NOT

bool bothTrue = isTrue && isFalse; // Logical AND

bool eitherTrue = isTrue || isFalse; // Logical OR
```

Control Structures

Dart supports various control structures for decision-making and looping:

- if, else if, else: Conditional statements.
- switch, case, default: Switch statements.
- for, while, do-while: Looping statements.

Here's an example of an if statement:

```
int age = 25;

if (age >= 18) {

print("You are an adult.");

} else {

print("You are not an adult.");

}
```

Conclusion

This is just a glimpse of Dart's syntax and basic elements. As you continue to explore Dart, you'll encounter more advanced features like functions, classes, and asynchronous programming. Understanding these fundamentals is essential for building robust Dart applications, whether you're working on web development, mobile app development with Flutter, or other Dart-based projects.

1.4 Dart and the Web: Why It Matters

Dart is not just another programming language; it has a significant impact on web development. In this section, we'll explore why Dart matters in the context of web development and what makes it a compelling choice for building web applications.

Performance

One of the key reasons Dart matters for web development is its performance. Dart is designed to be fast, and it's compiled to highly optimized JavaScript code that runs efficiently in modern web browsers. This means that Dart-based web applications can provide a smoother user experience and faster load times, making them competitive in the world of web development.

Developer Productivity

Dart's clean and expressive syntax, as well as its optional static typing, contribute to developer productivity. With strong tooling support, including code completion, type checking, and error detection, developers can write and maintain code more efficiently. This results in shorter development cycles and fewer runtime errors, ultimately saving time and resources.

Code Reusability

Dart's ability to run on both the client (browser) and server (Dart's own runtime environment, called DartVM) opens up opportunities for code reuse. Developers can share code and business logic between the frontend and backend of web applications, reducing duplication and ensuring consistency. This can lead to more maintainable and scalable web projects.

Web Components and Libraries

Dart comes with a rich set of libraries and packages that simplify common web development tasks. For example, the dart:html library allows developers to interact with the Document Object Model (DOM) and manipulate web page elements seamlessly. Additionally, Dart provides libraries for handling asynchronous programming, HTTP requests, and much more, reducing the need for external dependencies.

Strongly Typed Language

Dart's optional static typing allows developers to catch type-related errors at compile time, providing an extra layer of safety when building web applications. This can lead to more robust and stable web projects, as type-related issues are discovered and resolved early in the development process.

Frameworks and Tools

Dart has its own ecosystem of web development tools and frameworks, with Flutter being one of the most notable. Flutter allows developers to build not only web applications but also mobile apps for Android and iOS using a single codebase. This level of code reuse and the ability to target multiple platforms with a single technology stack is a significant advantage.

Growing Community

Over the years, Dart has gained traction in the web development community. It has an active and growing community of developers, which means more resources, libraries, and support are available. As Dart continues to evolve, its ecosystem becomes stronger and more reliable for web development.

In summary, Dart matters in web development due to its performance, developer productivity, code reusability, rich libraries, strong typing, frameworks like Flutter, and a growing community. Whether you're building modern web applications or exploring cross-platform development with Flutter, Dart provides a versatile and powerful toolkit for web development projects of all sizes.

1.5 The Dart Community: Resources and Support

The Dart programming language has a vibrant and supportive community that plays a crucial role in its growth and adoption. In this section, we'll explore the resources and support available within the Dart community and how they can benefit developers.

Official Documentation

The Dart team maintains comprehensive and well-structured official documentation available at dart.dev[3]. The documentation covers everything from language basics to advanced topics, libraries, and tools. Whether you're a beginner or an experienced developer, the official documentation is an invaluable resource for learning and reference.

Dart Pub

Dart Pub[4] is the official package repository for Dart. It hosts thousands of packages contributed by the community, ranging from utility libraries to full-fledged frameworks and tools. You can search for packages, view their documentation, and easily include them in your Dart projects using the Dart package manager (pub).

3. https://dart.dev/

4. https://pub.dev/

Dart GitHub Repository

The Dart language and its ecosystem are open source, and their development takes place on GitHub. You can find the official Dart GitHub repository at github.com/dart-lang. It's not only a place to view the source code but also an avenue for reporting issues, contributing to the language and its tools, and staying updated on the latest developments.

Dart Dev Community

The Dart Dev community is a place where Dart developers come together to share knowledge, ask questions, and discuss various topics related to Dart and its ecosystem. You can join the community at groups.google.com/g/dart-dev.

Stack Overflow

Stack Overflow is a popular platform for asking and answering technical questions, and it has a dedicated dart tag. Many developers turn to Stack Overflow when they encounter challenges or need help with Dart-related issues. It's an excellent resource for troubleshooting and learning from others in the community.

Dart Gitter Chat

For real-time discussions and quick questions, the Dart Gitter chat room is a valuable resource. You can join the chat at gitter.im/dart-lang/community and connect with other Dart developers from around the world.

Conferences and Meetups

The Dart community organizes conferences, meetups, and events where developers can network, learn from experts, and share their experiences. Keep an eye out for Dart-related events in your region or participate in virtual conferences to stay connected with the community.

Dart Blog and Twitter

To stay updated on Dart's latest news, announcements, and articles, you can follow the official Dart Blog at dart.dev/blog and the Dart Twitter account @dart_lang. These sources provide insights into the language's development and community activities.

Online Tutorials and Courses

Numerous online tutorials, courses, and video content are available for learning Dart. These resources cater to learners of all levels, from beginners to advanced developers. Platforms like YouTube and Udemy host Dart-related content that can help you expand your knowledge and skills.

Local User Groups

Depending on your location, you may find local Dart user groups or meetups. These gatherings provide opportunities to connect with developers in your area, share experiences, and learn from one another. Check if there are any Dart-related events happening in your vicinity.

In conclusion, the Dart community offers a wealth of resources, support, and opportunities for developers. Whether you're seeking documentation, packages, help with issues, or simply want to connect with other Dart enthusiasts, the Dart community provides a welcoming and collaborative environment to enhance your Dart programming journey.

Chapter 2: Basic Concepts in Dart

2.1 Variables and Data Types

In Dart, variables are used to store and manipulate data. Understanding variables and data types is fundamental to writing Dart code. Let's delve into this essential topic.

Declaring Variables

You can declare a variable in Dart using the var keyword, followed by the variable name and an optional type annotation. Dart allows you to omit the type annotation and relies on type inference:

var name = 'Alice'; // Inferred as String

var age = 30; // Inferred as int

In this example, Dart infers the data types based on the assigned values. name is inferred as a String, and age is inferred as an int.

You can also explicitly specify the data type:

String greeting = 'Hello'; // Explicitly specifying String

int score = 100; // Explicitly specifying int

Dynamic Type

Dart provides the dynamic type, which allows a variable to hold values of any type. This flexibility can be useful in certain situations, but it comes at the cost of losing type safety:

dynamic dynamicVariable = 'I can hold a String';

dynamicVariable = 42; // Now I can hold an int

dynamicVariable = true; // Now I can hold a bool

While dynamic can be powerful, it's recommended to use it sparingly, as it can lead to runtime errors if not used carefully.

Constants

In Dart, you can declare constants using the final and const keywords. Constants are variables whose values cannot be changed after they are assigned:

final String language = 'Dart'; // A final variable

const int daysInAWeek = 7; // A const variable

The difference between final and const is that final allows the value to be assigned at runtime, whereas const requires a value to be known at compile-time.

String Interpolation

String interpolation is a convenient way to embed values within a string. In Dart, you can use the ${expression} syntax to interpolate values into strings:

String name = 'Alice';

int age = 30;

print('My name is $name and I am $age years old.');

Dart automatically converts the expressions inside ${} to their string representations and inserts them into the string.

Type Conversions

Dart allows you to convert between different data types using type casting. For example, you can convert a double to an int using the .toInt() method:

double pi = 3.14159265359;

int approximation = pi.toInt(); // Converts double to int

Similarly, you can convert an int to a double using the .toDouble() method.

Null Safety

Starting with Dart 2.12, Dart introduced null safety, which helps prevent null reference errors. In Dart, variables are considered non-nullable by default, meaning they cannot hold null values unless explicitly declared as nullable using the ? symbol:

String? nullableString = null; // Nullable variable

String nonNullableString = 'Dart'; // Non-nullable variable

This feature enhances code safety and readability by making it clear which variables can contain null values.

In summary, variables and data types are the building blocks of Dart programming. Understanding how to declare variables, use different data types, work with constants, perform type conversions, and utilize null safety are essential skills for writing Dart code efficiently and safely. These concepts lay the foundation for more advanced Dart programming topics covered in later chapters.

2.2 Control Flow: Making Decisions in Dart

Control flow structures allow you to make decisions and control the flow of your Dart programs. In this section, we'll explore the essential control flow constructs in Dart, including conditionals and loops.

Conditional Statements

Conditional statements in Dart allow you to execute different code blocks based on conditions. The most common conditional statement is the if statement:

```
int age = 20;

if (age >= 18) {

print('You are an adult.');

} else {

print('You are not an adult.');

}
```

In this example, the code inside the curly braces {} following if is executed only if the condition (age >= 18) is true. Otherwise, the code inside the else block is executed.

Dart also provides the else if clause for handling multiple conditions:

```
int score = 75;

if (score >= 90) {

print('A');

} else if (score >= 80) {
```

```
print('B');
} else if (score >= 70) {
print('C');
} else {
print('D');
}
```

Here, the code evaluates the conditions in order, and the first condition that is true triggers the corresponding code block.

Switch Statements

Dart offers the switch statement for handling multiple possible values or cases. It provides a cleaner alternative to a series of if-else if statements:

```
String day = 'Monday';
switch (day) {
case 'Monday':
print('It\'s the start of the workweek.');
break;
case 'Friday':
print('It\'s almost the weekend!');
break;
default:
```

```
print('It\'s a regular day.');
}
```

The break keyword is used to exit the switch statement after a case is matched. If no cases match, the code in the default block is executed.

Loops

Loops allow you to repeat a block of code multiple times. Dart supports several types of loops, including for, while, and do-while loops.

For Loop

The for loop is commonly used when you know the number of iterations in advance:

```
for (int i = 1; i <= 5; i++) {
print('Iteration $i');
}
```

In this example, the loop initializes a counter variable i, checks the condition (i <= 5), and increments i after each iteration.

While Loop

The while loop continues executing as long as a specified condition is true:

```
int count = 0;
while (count < 5) {
```

```
print('Count: $count');
count++;
}
```

The code within the while block runs repeatedly as long as the condition (count < 5) is true.

Do-While Loop

The do-while loop is similar to the while loop, but it always executes the code block at least once before checking the condition:

```
int number = 1;
do {
print('Number: $number');
number++;
} while (number <= 5);
```

In this example, the code block is executed first, and then the condition (number <= 5) is checked.

Breaking and Continuing Loops

In Dart, you can use the break statement to exit a loop prematurely and the continue statement to skip the current iteration and move to the next one:

```
for (int i = 1; i <= 5; i++) {
if (i == 3) {
```

```
continue; // Skip iteration 3

}

if (i == 4) {

break; // Exit the loop at iteration 4

}

print('Iteration $i');

}
```

These control flow constructs enable you to create more dynamic and efficient programs by controlling the flow of execution based on conditions and looping as needed. Understanding and using conditionals and loops effectively is a crucial part of Dart programming and software development in general.

2.3 Functions and Methods: Basics

Functions and methods are essential in Dart as they allow you to encapsulate reusable blocks of code. In this section, we'll explore the basics of defining and using functions and methods in Dart.

Defining Functions

In Dart, you can define a function using the function_name(parameters) { /* code */ } syntax. Here's a simple example of a function that adds two numbers and returns the result:

```
int add(int a, int b) {

return a + b;

}
```

```
void main() {

int result = add(5, 3);

print('The sum is $result');

}
```

In this example, the add function takes two integer parameters (a and b) and returns their sum. The main function calls the add function with arguments 5 and 3, stores the result in the result variable, and then prints the result.

Function Parameters

Dart functions can have parameters, which are variables that receive values when the function is called. Parameters allow you to pass data into functions and make them more versatile. Here's an example of a function with parameters:

```
void greet(String name) {

print('Hello, $name!');

}

void main() {

greet('Alice');

greet('Bob');

}
```

The greet function takes a String parameter name, which is used to personalize the greeting message.

Return Values

Functions in Dart can return values using the return keyword. The return type of a function is specified before the function name. Here's an example of a function that calculates the area of a rectangle and returns the result:

```
double calculateRectangleArea(double length, double width) {

double area = length * width;

return area;

}

void main() {

double length = 5.0;

double width = 3.0;

double area = calculateRectangleArea(length, width);

print('The area is $area square units');

}
```

In this example, the calculateRectangleArea function returns a double value representing the area of the rectangle.

Optional Parameters

Dart allows you to define optional parameters in functions by enclosing them in square brackets []. Optional parameters can have default values, making them optional to provide when calling the function. Here's an example:

```
String greet(String name, {String? greeting = 'Hello'}) {
```

```
return '$greeting, $name!';

}

void main() {

print(greet('Alice'));

print(greet('Bob', greeting: 'Hi'));

}
```

In this example, the greet function has an optional parameter greeting, which defaults to 'Hello' if not provided. When calling the function, you can specify the greeting value using named parameters.

Anonymous Functions (Closures)

Dart supports anonymous functions, also known as closures. These are functions without a name that can be assigned to variables or passed as arguments to other functions. Here's an example of an anonymous function:

```
void main() {

// Anonymous function assigned to a variable

var add = (int a, int b) {

return a + b;

};

int result = add(5, 3);

print('The sum is $result');

}
```

In this example, we define an anonymous function and assign it to the add variable. The function can then be called just like any other function.

Method

A method is a function that is associated with a class or object. In Dart, methods are defined within classes and can access the properties and behavior of the class. Here's a simple example of a class with a method:

```
class Calculator {

int add(int a, int b) {

return a + b;

}

}

void main() {

Calculator calculator = Calculator();

int result = calculator.add(5, 3);

print('The sum is $result');

}
```

In this example, we define a Calculator class with an add method. We then create an instance of the Calculator class and call its add method to perform the addition.

Functions and methods are foundational concepts in Dart, enabling code organization, reusability, and encapsulation. Understanding how to define, use, and pass functions as arguments is crucial for building complex Dart applications.

2.4 Collections: Lists, Maps, and Sets

Collections are essential for storing and managing multiple values in Dart. Dart provides three primary types of collections: lists, maps, and sets. In this section, we'll explore these collection types and how to work with them.

Lists

A list in Dart is an ordered collection of elements. Lists can contain elements of any data type, including other lists. Here's how you can create and work with lists:

```
// Creating a list of integers

List<int> numbers = [1, 2, 3, 4, 5];

// Accessing elements

int firstNumber = numbers[0]; // Accessing the first element (index 0)

// Modifying elements

numbers[2] = 10; // Modifying the third element (index 2)

// Adding elements to the end of the list

numbers.add(6);

// Removing elements

numbers.remove(4); // Removes the element with value 4
```

```
// Finding the length of the list

int length = numbers.length;

// Iterating through a list

for (int number in numbers) {

print(number);

}
```

In this example, we create a list of integers, access elements by index, modify elements, add elements, remove elements, and find the length of the list. Lists are versatile and can be used in a wide range of scenarios.

Maps

A map in Dart is an unordered collection of key-value pairs. Each key is unique, and it maps to a specific value. Maps are often used to represent data with associated attributes. Here's how you can create and work with maps:

```
// Creating a map of user information

Map<String, dynamic> user = {

'name': 'Alice',

'age': 30,

'isStudent': false,

};

// Accessing values by key
```

```
String name = user['name']; // Accessing the 'name' key

// Modifying values

user['age'] = 31; // Modifying the 'age' value

// Adding new key-value pairs

user['country'] = 'USA';

// Removing key-value pairs

user.remove('isStudent');

// Checking if a key exists

bool hasCountry = user.containsKey('country');

// Getting a list of keys and values

List<String> keys = user.keys.toList();

List<dynamic> values = user.values.toList();

// Iterating through a map

user.forEach((key, value) {

print('$key: $value');

});
```

In this example, we create a map representing user information, access values by key, modify values, add key-value pairs, remove key-value pairs, check for key existence, and iterate through the map.

Sets

A set in Dart is an unordered collection of unique elements. Sets are useful when you need to ensure that a collection contains only distinct values. Here's how you can create and work with sets:

```
// Creating a set of integers

Set<int> uniqueNumbers = {1, 2, 3, 4, 5};

// Adding elements to the set

uniqueNumbers.add(6);

// Removing elements

uniqueNumbers.remove(4);

// Checking if an element exists

bool containsFive = uniqueNumbers.contains(5);

// Finding the size of the set

int size = uniqueNumbers.length;

// Iterating through a set

for (int number in uniqueNumbers) {

print(number);

}
```

In this example, we create a set of integers, add elements, remove elements, check for element existence, find the size of the set, and iterate through the set. Sets are ideal when you want to maintain a unique collection of values.

Collections are a crucial part of Dart programming, enabling you to work with structured data efficiently. Depending on your specific requirements, you can choose between lists, maps, and sets to organize and manipulate your data effectively. Understanding these collection types and their operations is essential for many Dart applications.

2.5 Error Handling and Exceptions

Error handling is a crucial aspect of writing robust Dart applications. In Dart, exceptions are used to handle errors and unexpected situations gracefully. In this section, we'll explore how to work with exceptions and handle errors effectively.

Exceptions in Dart

An exception is an event that occurs during the execution of a program and disrupts the normal flow of instructions. Dart provides a variety of built-in exception classes, and you can also create custom exceptions to handle specific scenarios.

Here are some common exceptions in Dart:

- FormatException: Raised when a string cannot be parsed as expected, such as when converting a non-numeric string to an integer.

- RangeError: Raised when an index or value is out of a valid range, such as accessing an index that doesn't exist in a list.

- ArgumentError: Raised when an invalid argument is passed to a function or method.

- NoSuchMethodError: Raised when a method or function is called on an object that doesn't support it.
- TypeError: Raised when a value has an unexpected type.

Throwing Exceptions

In Dart, you can throw an exception using the throw keyword followed by an exception object. For example, to throw a RangeError when accessing an invalid index in a list:

```
List<int> numbers = [1, 2, 3];

try {

int invalidNumber = numbers[5]; // Accessing an invalid index

} catch (e) {

print('Error: $e');

}
```

In this example, the try block attempts to access an invalid index, which raises a RangeError. The catch block catches the exception and prints an error message.

Catching Exceptions

To catch and handle exceptions, you can use try and catch blocks. Dart allows you to catch exceptions of specific types and handle them differently. Here's an example:

```
try {

int result = 5 ~/ 0; // Division by zero
```

```
} on IntegerDivisionByZeroException {

print('Cannot divide by zero.');

} catch (e) {

print('An error occurred: $e');

}
```

In this code, we attempt to perform a division by zero, which raises an IntegerDivisionByZeroException. We catch this specific exception type and handle it by printing a custom error message. If any other type of exception occurs, it will be caught by the generic catch block.

Finally Block

You can use a finally block in combination with try and catch to specify code that runs regardless of whether an exception is thrown or not. This is useful for cleanup operations or ensuring that certain code always executes:

```
try {

// Code that may throw an exception

} catch (e) {

// Handling the exception

} finally {

// Code that always runs, whether an exception occurred or not

}
```

Rethrowing Exceptions

In some cases, you may want to catch an exception and then rethrow it to allow it to propagate to a higher-level handler. Dart allows you to rethrow an exception using the rethrow keyword:

```
try {

// Code that may throw an exception

} catch (e) {

print('An error occurred: $e');

rethrow; // Rethrow the exception

}
```

This can be useful when you want to log or handle an exception at a specific level of your application but still want it to be handled by a higher-level exception handler.

Custom Exceptions

You can create custom exception classes by extending the built-in Exception class or any other existing exception class. Custom exceptions allow you to provide meaningful error messages and specific exception types for your application's needs:

```
class CustomException implements Exception {

final String message;

CustomException(this.message);

@override

String toString() => 'CustomException: $message';
```

```
}

void main() {

try {

throw CustomException('This is a custom exception.');

} catch (e) {

print('Caught an exception: $e');

}

}
```

In this example, we define a custom exception class CustomException that extends Exception. We provide a custom error message and override the toString method to display the exception message.

Error handling and exceptions are essential for building reliable and robust Dart applications. By understanding how to throw, catch, and handle exceptions, you can gracefully manage unexpected situations and provide meaningful error messages to users and developers.

Chapter 3: Advanced Dart Programming

3.1 Object-Oriented Programming in Dart

Object-Oriented Programming (OOP) is a programming paradigm that focuses on organizing code into reusable and structured objects. Dart is an object-oriented language, and in this section, we'll explore the principles and concepts of OOP in Dart.

Classes and Objects

In Dart, everything is an object. Objects are instances of classes, which serve as blueprints for creating objects. Classes define the structure and behavior of objects. Here's a basic example of a class definition in Dart:

```
class Person {

String name;

int age;

// Constructor

Person(this.name, this.age);

// Method

void sayHello() {

print('Hello, my name is $name and I am $age years old.');

}

}
```

In this example, we define a Person class with two instance variables (name and age), a constructor that initializes these variables, and a method sayHello that prints a greeting.

To create an object (an instance) of the Person class:

```
void main() {

Person alice = Person('Alice', 30);

alice.sayHello();

}
```

Here, we create an instance of the Person class named alice and call its sayHello method.

Encapsulation

Encapsulation is one of the key principles of OOP and involves bundling data (variables) and methods (functions) that operate on that data into a single unit, known as a class. In Dart, you can control access to class members (variables and methods) using access modifiers:

- public: Members with no access modifier are considered public and can be accessed from anywhere.
- private: Members prefixed with an underscore _ are considered private and can only be accessed from within the same class.

```
class Circle {

double _radius; // Private variable

Circle(this._radius); // Constructor
```

```
double calculateArea() {

return 3.14 * _radius * _radius; // Accessing private variable

}

}
```

In this example, the _radius variable is private, and the calculateArea method can access it.

Inheritance

Inheritance allows you to create a new class (subclass or derived class) based on an existing class (superclass or base class). Dart supports single inheritance, meaning a class can inherit from one superclass. Here's an example:

```
class Animal {

void speak() {

print('Animal speaks');

}

}

class Dog extends Animal {

@override

void speak() {

print('Dog barks');

}

}
```

In this example, the Dog class extends the Animal class and overrides its speak method. This allows the Dog class to have its own implementation of the speak method.

Polymorphism

Polymorphism allows objects of different classes to be treated as objects of a common superclass. It enables code to work with objects in a generic way, without needing to know their specific types. In Dart, polymorphism is achieved through method overriding and interfaces (abstract classes). Here's an example of polymorphism using method overriding:

```
class Shape {
double area() {
return 0.0;
}
}
class Circle extends Shape {
double radius;
Circle(this.radius);
@override
double area() {
return 3.14 * radius * radius;
}
}
```

```
class Rectangle extends Shape {
double width;
double height;
Rectangle(this.width, this.height);
@override
double area() {
return width * height;
}
}
```

In this example, the Shape class defines a common area method, and both Circle and Rectangle classes override this method to provide their own implementations.

Abstraction and Interfaces

Abstraction is the process of hiding the complex implementation details and showing only the necessary features of an object. In Dart, you can achieve abstraction using abstract classes and interfaces. An abstract class cannot be instantiated but can be used as a base for other classes:

```
abstract class Animal {
void speak();
}
class Dog extends Animal {
```

```
@override

void speak() {

print('Dog barks');

}

}
```

In this example, the Animal class is abstract and defines an abstract method speak. The Dog class inherits from Animal and provides an implementation for the speak method.

Getters and Setters

In Dart, you can use getters and setters to access and manipulate the private properties of an object. Getters are used to retrieve the value of a property, while setters are used to modify it. Here's an example:

```
class Temperature {

double _celsius;

Temperature(this._celsius);

double get celsius => _celsius;

set celsius(double value) {

if (value >= -273.15) {

_celsius = value;

}

}

double get fahrenheit => (_celsius * 9 / 5) + 32;
```

```
}
```

In this example, the Temperature class has a private _celsius property, and it provides getters and setters for both Celsius and Fahrenheit temperatures.

Object-Oriented Programming is a fundamental paradigm for organizing code, promoting reusability, and modeling real-world entities in Dart applications. Understanding the concepts of classes, objects, encapsulation, inheritance, polymorphism, abstraction, and getters/setters is essential for effective OOP in Dart. These principles enable developers to create well-structured and maintainable code.

3.2 Understanding Async Programming and Futures

Async programming is a fundamental aspect of modern software development, especially when dealing with tasks that may take time, such as network requests or file operations. Dart provides robust support for asynchronous programming through features like Futures and the async and await keywords. In this section, we'll dive into the concepts of async programming in Dart.

Asynchronous vs. Synchronous Code

In synchronous code, each operation is executed one after the other, blocking the program's execution until the current operation completes. This can lead to performance issues and unresponsiveness in applications that need to perform time-consuming tasks.

Async programming, on the other hand, allows your program to perform multiple tasks concurrently without blocking the main thread. It enables non-blocking operations, making your application more responsive and efficient.

Futures in Dart

A Future in Dart represents a potential value or error that will be available at some time in the future. Futures are commonly used to handle asynchronous operations, such as reading data from a file or making an HTTP request. You can think of a Future as a placeholder for a value that will be computed later.

Here's an example of using a Future to simulate a delayed operation:

```
Future<int> fetchUserData() {

return Future.delayed(Duration(seconds: 2), () => 42);

}

void main() {

print('Fetching user data...');

fetchUserData().then((result) {

print('User data fetched: $result');

});

print('Program continues...');

}
```

In this example, fetchUserData returns a Future<int> that resolves to 42 after a 2-second delay. We use the then method to specify what to do when the Future completes.

async and await

The async and await keywords simplify asynchronous code and make it look more like synchronous code. The async keyword is used to mark a function as asynchronous, and the await keyword is used inside an async function to wait for a Future to complete.

Here's an example of using async and await to fetch user data:

```
Future<int> fetchUserData() async {

await Future.delayed(Duration(seconds: 2));

return 42;

}

void main() async {

print('Fetching user data...');

final result = await fetchUserData();

print('User data fetched: $result');

print('Program continues...');

}
```

In this code, fetchUserData is marked as async, and we use await to wait for the Future to complete. This makes the code more readable and resembles synchronous code.

Error Handling with Futures

Futures allow you to handle errors gracefully. You can use the catchError method or the try-catch block to handle errors that occur during the execution of a Future. Here's an example:

```
Future<int> divide(int a, int b) async {

if (b == 0) {
```

```
throw Exception('Division by zero');
}
return a ~/ b;
}
void main() async {
try {
final result = await divide(10, 0);
print('Result: $result');
} catch (e) {
print('Error: $e');
}
}
```

In this example, the divide function throws an exception if the divisor b is zero. We catch the exception in the try-catch block and handle it appropriately.

Concurrent Asynchronous Operations

Dart allows you to run multiple asynchronous operations concurrently and wait for all of them to complete using Future.wait. This is useful when you need to perform multiple asynchronous tasks in parallel. Here's an example:

```
Future<int> fetchUserData() async {
await Future.delayed(Duration(seconds: 2));
```

```
return 42;
}
Future<String> fetchNews() async {
await Future.delayed(Duration(seconds: 3));
return 'Latest news';
}
void main() async {
print('Fetching data...');
final results = await Future.wait([fetchUserData(), fetchNews()]);
final userData = results[0];
final news = results[1];
print('User data: $userData, News: $news');
}
```

In this code, we use Future.wait to run fetchUserData and fetchNews concurrently and wait for both to complete before continuing.

Async programming is essential for building responsive and efficient Dart applications. Understanding how to work with Futures, async, and await allows you to handle asynchronous operations gracefully and write code that is more responsive and user-friendly.

3.3 Advanced Collections and Iterables

Dart provides a rich set of collection classes and powerful iterable operations that allow you to work with data in a flexible and efficient way. In this section, we will explore some advanced collections and the iterable operations available in Dart.

Advanced Collections

LinkedHashSet

A LinkedHashSet is similar to a Set but maintains the insertion order of elements. This can be useful when you need to keep track of the order in which elements were added to the collection.

```
import 'dart:collection';

void main() {

LinkedHashSet<String> countries = LinkedHashSet<String>();

countries.add("USA");

countries.add("Canada");

countries.add("Mexico");

print(countries); // Output: {USA, Canada, Mexico}

}
```

In this example, the LinkedHashSet preserves the order of elements, so the output will be in the order in which elements were added.

Queue

A Queue is a double-ended queue that allows efficient insertion and removal of elements from both ends. You can use it for implementing a queue or a deque (double-ended queue).

```
import 'dart:collection';

void main() {

Queue<String> queue = Queue<String>();

queue.addFirst("First");

queue.addLast("Last");

print(queue); // Output: (First, Last)

String firstItem = queue.removeFirst();

print(firstItem); // Output: First

}
```

In this example, we use a Queue to add elements at both ends and remove the first element.

Iterable Operations

Dart provides a set of powerful iterable operations that allow you to manipulate and process collections easily. These operations can be used on lists, sets, maps, and other iterable objects.

map()

The map() operation applies a given function to each element of the collection and returns a new iterable containing the results.

```
void main() {

List<int> numbers = [1, 2, 3, 4, 5];
```

```
List<int> squaredNumbers = numbers.map((int x) => x * x).toList();

print(squaredNumbers); // Output: [1, 4, 9, 16, 25]

}
```

In this example, map() is used to square each element of the numbers list.

where()

The where() operation filters elements in the collection based on a given condition and returns a new iterable with the elements that satisfy the condition.

```
void main() {

List<int> numbers = [1, 2, 3, 4, 5];

List<int> evenNumbers = numbers.where((int x) => x % 2 == 0).toList();

print(evenNumbers); // Output: [2, 4]

}
```

Here, where() filters out the odd numbers from the numbers list.

reduce()

The reduce() operation combines the elements of a collection into a single value by repeatedly applying a binary operation. It takes an initial value and a combining function.

```
void main() {
```

```
List<int> numbers = [1, 2, 3, 4, 5];

int sum = numbers.reduce((int value, int element) => value + element);

print(sum); // Output: 15

}
```

In this example, reduce() is used to find the sum of all elements in the numbers list.

forEach()

The forEach() operation applies a given function to each element in the collection. It doesn't return a new iterable but is useful for performing actions on each element.

```
void main() {

List<String> names = ['Alice', 'Bob', 'Charlie'];

names.forEach((name) {

print('Hello, $name!');

});

// Output:

// Hello, Alice!

// Hello, Bob!

// Hello, Charlie!

}
```

Here, forEach() is used to print a greeting message for each name in the names list.

These are just a few examples of the iterable operations available in Dart. These operations make it easy to perform various transformations and operations on collections, simplifying your code and making it more expressive.

3.4 Generics: Types and Collections

Generics are a powerful feature in Dart that allow you to write code that works with different types while providing type safety. Generics enable you to create classes, functions, and collections that can work with a variety of data types without sacrificing type checking. In this section, we'll explore how generics work in Dart and their use in collections.

Introduction to Generics

Generics in Dart are denoted by type parameters enclosed in angle brackets <T>, where T is a placeholder for the actual data type. You can define generic classes, functions, and interfaces, and the type parameter T can be used throughout the code to represent the actual type.

Here's a simple example of a generic class:

```
class Box<T> {

T value;

Box(this.value);

}

void main() {
```

```
var intBox = Box<int>(42);
var stringBox = Box<String>('Dart');
print(intBox.value); // Output: 42
print(stringBox.value); // Output: Dart
}
```

In this example, Box is a generic class that can hold values of any data type. We create instances of Box with different type parameters, and the type parameter T is used to specify the data type of the value property.

Generic Functions

You can also create generic functions in Dart. These functions can work with different types, and the type parameter is specified similarly to generic classes.

```
T findMax<T extends Comparable<T>>(List<T> list) {
if (list.isEmpty) {
throw ArgumentError('List cannot be empty.');
}
T max = list[0];
for (var item in list) {
if (item.compareTo(max) > 0) {
max = item;
}
```

```
}

return max;

}

void main() {

var numbers = [5, 3, 9, 2, 8];

var words = ['apple', 'banana', 'cherry', 'date'];

var maxNumber = findMax(numbers);

var maxWord = findMax(words);

print('Max number: $maxNumber'); // Output: Max number: 9

print('Max word: $maxWord'); // Output: Max word: cherry

}
```

In this example, findMax is a generic function that finds the maximum value in a list of comparable elements. The type parameter T is constrained to types that extend the Comparable interface to ensure that comparisons are possible.

Generic Collections

Dart provides several generic collections in its standard library, such as List<T>, Set<T>, and Map<K, V>. These collections can hold elements of specific types and offer type safety.

```
void main() {

List<int> numbers = [1, 2, 3, 4, 5];

Set<String> names = {'Alice', 'Bob', 'Charlie'};
```

```
Map<String, int> scores = {'Alice': 95, 'Bob': 87, 'Charlie': 92};

// Type safety enforced by generics

numbers.add(6); // Valid

// numbers.add('seven'); // Error: The argument type 'String' can't be assigned to the parameter type 'int'.

print(numbers); // Output: [1, 2, 3, 4, 5, 6]

print(names); // Output: {Alice, Bob, Charlie}

print(scores); // Output: {Alice: 95, Bob: 87, Charlie: 92}

}
```

In this code, the use of generics ensures that only elements of the specified types can be added to the collections. Attempting to add an element of the wrong type will result in a compile-time error.

Generics provide a powerful tool for writing flexible and type-safe code in Dart. They allow you to create reusable classes and functions that work with different data types while maintaining type safety. Generics are widely used in Dart's standard library and are essential for writing clean and efficient code.

3.5 Effective Dart: Best Practices

Effective Dart is a set of best practices and guidelines recommended by the Dart language team to help you write clean, maintainable, and efficient Dart code. Following these best practices can lead to improved code quality and a better development experience. In this section, we'll explore some of the key recommendations and practices outlined in Effective Dart.

Code Formatting

Consistent code formatting is essential for code readability and maintainability. Dart provides the dartfmt tool, which automatically formats your code according to the Dart style guide. It's a good practice to run dartfmt on your code before committing it.

To format your Dart code using dartfmt, you can run the following command:

```
dartfmt -w .
```

The -w flag stands for "write," which means it will apply the formatting changes to your code.

Effective Use of Linter Rules

Dart provides a set of static analysis rules to catch potential issues and improve code quality. You can enable these rules by using the Dart Analyzer or by configuring your project's analysis_options.yaml file.

For example, the prefer_final_fields rule suggests making class fields final if they are never reassigned after being initialized. This can improve code safety and clarity:

```
class Person {

final String name;

final int age;

Person(this.name, this.age);

}
```

In this example, the fields name and age are marked as final because they are not reassigned after being initialized in the constructor.

Effective Use of Asynchronous Code

When working with asynchronous code in Dart, it's important to handle errors gracefully and use the await keyword appropriately. Effective Dart recommends using the try-catch block to handle exceptions when awaiting a Future.

```
void fetchData() async {

try {

final data = await fetchDataFromNetwork();

// Process data

} catch (e) {

// Handle error

print('An error occurred: $e');

}

}
```

In this code, the try-catch block ensures that any errors thrown during the asynchronous operation are caught and can be handled appropriately.

Effective Use of Comments

Effective Dart suggests using comments effectively to document your code and provide context to readers. Comments should be clear and concise. Use comments to explain the why, not just the how, of your code.

```
// Calculate the total price
double calculateTotal(List<double> prices) {
double total = 0;
for (var price in prices) {
total += price;
}
return total;
}
```

In this example, the comment provides context about the purpose of the function.

Effective Use of Named Constructors

Named constructors are a useful feature in Dart that allows you to provide multiple ways to create instances of a class. Effective Dart recommends using named constructors for clarity and to provide meaningful ways to initialize objects.

```
class Point {
double x;
double y;
Point(this.x, this.y);
Point.origin() {
```

```
x = 0;

y = 0;

}

}
```

In this code, the Point.origin() named constructor provides a clear way to create a Point with coordinates at the origin (0, 0).

These are just a few examples of best practices and recommendations from Effective Dart. Following these guidelines can lead to more maintainable and readable code, making your Dart projects more enjoyable to work on and collaborate with others. Be sure to consult the official Effective Dart documentation for more details and best practices.

Chapter 4: Dart and Web Development

4.1 Introduction to Web Programming with Dart

Dart is a versatile language that extends beyond server-side and mobile app development to web programming. With the advent of Dart for the web, you can build web applications using Dart that are both efficient and maintainable. In this section, we'll introduce you to web programming with Dart and explore its features and benefits.

Dart for Web Development

Dart's journey into web development began with the development of the Dart language itself and the creation of Dartium, a custom build of Chromium with a Dart virtual machine. Dart was initially designed to be executed in the browser. However, as the web ecosystem evolved, Dart's focus shifted towards transpiling Dart code into JavaScript to run in all modern web browsers.

One of the main advantages of using Dart for web development is its consistency. Dart allows you to use the same language and libraries for both the client and server sides of web applications, thanks to server-side frameworks like Aqueduct and Shelf.

Building Web Apps with Dart

To start building web applications with Dart, you'll need a Dart development environment set up. You can use the Dart SDK and tools like the Dartium browser for development. Additionally, popular IDEs like Visual Studio Code offer Dart support through extensions.

Dart web applications are typically organized into packages and use the Pub package manager to manage dependencies. You can create a new Dart web project using the webdev tool, which simplifies tasks like building and serving web applications.

```
# Create a new Dart web project

webdev create my_web_app
```

Once your project is set up, you can write Dart code that gets transpiled into JavaScript for the web. Dart's syntax is concise and familiar to many developers, making it easy to learn and use.

The Dart SDK for the Web

The Dart SDK provides a set of libraries and tools for web development. The dart:html library allows you to interact with the Document Object Model (DOM) and create dynamic web applications. You can manipulate HTML elements, handle events, and perform tasks such as making HTTP requests.

Here's an example of using dart:html to manipulate the DOM:

```
import 'dart:html';

void main() {

var button = ButtonElement()..text = 'Click Me';

var output = DivElement();

button.onClick.listen((event) {

output.text = 'Button clicked!';

});
```

```
document.body!.children.addAll([button, output]);

}
```

In this code, we create an HTML button and a div element, attach a click event listener to the button, and manipulate the DOM to display a message when the button is clicked.

Transpiling to JavaScript

Dart code is transpiled into JavaScript for compatibility with web browsers. Dart provides tools like dart2js for this purpose. Transpilation ensures that your Dart code runs efficiently in all modern browsers.

```
# Transpile Dart code to JavaScript

dart2js -o main.dart.js main.dart
```

The resulting JavaScript code can be included in your HTML pages like any other JavaScript file.

Dart for web development offers a robust and efficient way to create modern web applications. Its consistency, concise syntax, and powerful libraries make it a compelling choice for both front-end and back-end development. In the next sections, we'll dive deeper into Dart's interaction with HTML, managing web APIs, building interactive web applications, and exploring web frameworks.

4.2 Dart and HTML: A Seamless Interaction

Dart provides a seamless interaction with HTML, making it easy to build dynamic web applications with rich user interfaces. In this section, we'll explore how Dart can be used to manipulate HTML elements, handle events, and create interactive web pages.

Dart and the DOM

The Document Object Model (DOM) represents the structure of an HTML document as a tree of objects. Dart's dart:html library provides classes and methods for interacting with the DOM. You can use Dart to manipulate HTML elements, modify their attributes, and respond to user interactions.

For example, you can use Dart to create new HTML elements and append them to the document:

```
import 'dart:html';

void main() {

// Create a new heading element

var heading = HeadingElement.h1()

..text = 'Hello, Dart and HTML';

// Append the heading to the body of the document

document.body!.children.add(heading);

}
```

In this code, we create an h1 element with the text "Hello, Dart and HTML" and append it to the document's body.

Event Handling

Dart allows you to handle events such as clicks, key presses, and form submissions easily. You can attach event listeners to HTML elements and respond to events with Dart functions.

```
import 'dart:html';
```

```
void main() {
var button = ButtonElement()..text = 'Click Me';
var output = ParagraphElement();
button.onClick.listen((MouseEvent event) {
output.text = 'Button clicked!';
});
document.body!.children.addAll([button, output]);
}
```

In this example, we create a button element and a paragraph element. We attach a click event listener to the button, and when the button is clicked, we update the paragraph's text.

Data Binding

Data binding is a powerful technique that allows you to keep the user interface in sync with your data model. Dart provides libraries like polymer.dart and angular.dart to implement data binding in web applications. These libraries make it easy to create components that automatically update when data changes.

Here's a simple example of data binding using polymer.dart:

```
import 'package:polymer/polymer.dart';
import 'dart:html';
@CustomTag('my-element')
class MyElement extends PolymerElement {
```

```
@published String message = 'Hello, Dart!';

MyElement.created() : super.created();

void changeMessage() {

message = 'New message!';

}

}
```

In this code, we define a custom element my-element with a property message. The @published annotation marks the property for data binding. When the changeMessage method is called, the message property is updated, and any bound elements automatically reflect the new value.

HTML Templates

HTML templates allow you to define reusable chunks of HTML that can be cloned and inserted into the document as needed. Dart provides a convenient way to work with templates using the TemplateElement class.

```
import 'dart:html';

void main() {

var template = TemplateElement()..innerHtml = '<p>Hello, Dart!</p>';

var clone = template.content.clone(true);

document.body!.children.add(clone);

}
```

In this example, we create an HTML template with a paragraph element. We then clone the template's content and append it to the document. Templates are useful for creating dynamic content and reusing HTML structures.

Dart's integration with HTML and the DOM provides a powerful foundation for building interactive web applications. Whether you're creating custom elements, handling events, implementing data binding, or working with HTML templates, Dart makes web development a seamless and enjoyable experience. The ability to use Dart on both the client and server sides further enhances its appeal for web application development.

4.3 Managing Web APIs and HTTP Requests

Web applications often need to interact with external services and APIs to fetch data, submit forms, or perform other actions. Dart provides powerful libraries for making HTTP requests and managing web APIs. In this section, we'll explore how to work with web APIs and handle HTTP requests in Dart.

The dart:html Library

Dart's dart:html library includes the HttpRequest class, which allows you to make HTTP requests to external servers and retrieve data. You can use this library to perform GET, POST, PUT, DELETE, and other HTTP methods.

Here's an example of making a simple GET request to fetch data from a server:

```
import 'dart:html';

void fetchData() {
```

```
HttpRequest.request('https://api.example.com/data',
method: 'GET',
requestHeaders: {'Authorization': 'Bearer YOUR_ACCESS_TOKEN'},
responseType: 'json').then((HttpRequest req) {
if (req.status == 200) {
print(req.responseText);
} else {
print('Request failed with status: ${req.status}');
}
}).catchError((error) {
print('Error occurred: $error');
});
}
```

In this code, we use HttpRequest.request to make a GET request to an API endpoint. We also set the request headers and specify the response type as JSON. The response is processed in the then callback, and errors are handled in the catchError callback.

The http Package

Dart offers the http package, which is a widely used package for making HTTP requests and handling responses. You can add this package to your Dart project's pubspec.yaml file and use it to simplify HTTP interactions.

```
dependencies:

http: ^0.13.3
```

Once you've added the package, you can use it to make HTTP requests like this:

```
import 'package:http/http.dart' as http;

void fetchData() async {

final response = await http.get(Uri.parse('https://api.example.com/data'));

if (response.statusCode == 200) {

print(response.body);

} else {

print('Request failed with status: ${response.statusCode}');

}

}
```

In this code, we import the http package and use it to make a GET request. The response is then checked for a successful status code (200) before processing the data.

Handling CORS

Cross-Origin Resource Sharing (CORS) is a security feature implemented by web browsers that restricts web pages from making requests to domains other than the one serving the web page. When working with web APIs, you may encounter CORS restrictions. To handle CORS, the API server needs to be configured to allow requests from your web domain, and you should use appropriate headers and options when making requests.

Authentication

When accessing protected resources on web APIs, you often need to include authentication tokens in your requests. Dart allows you to set headers for authentication, such as adding an Authorization header with a token.

```
import 'package:http/http.dart' as http;

void fetchData() async {

final headers = {'Authorization': 'Bearer YOUR_ACCESS_TOKEN'};

final response = await http.get(Uri.parse('https://api.example.com/data'),

headers: headers);

// Handle the response

}
```

In this example, we include an Authorization header with the access token in the HTTP request.

Error Handling

When making HTTP requests, it's essential to handle errors gracefully. You should handle network errors, server errors, and any other potential issues that may arise during the request.

```
import 'package:http/http.dart' as http;
```

```
void fetchData() async {
try {
final response = await http.get(Uri.parse('https://api.example.com/data'));
if (response.statusCode == 200) {
print(response.body);
} else {
print('Request failed with status: ${response.statusCode}');
}
} catch (error) {
print('Error occurred: $error');
}
}
```

In this code, we use a try-catch block to catch and handle errors that may occur during the HTTP request.

Handling web APIs and making HTTP requests is an essential part of web development, and Dart provides tools and libraries to streamline this process. Whether you choose to use the built-in dart:html library or third-party packages like http, Dart offers flexibility and options to meet your specific needs for web API interaction.

4.4 Building Interactive Web Applications

Building interactive web applications is a core part of web development, and Dart offers powerful features and libraries to help you create dynamic and engaging user interfaces. In this section, we'll explore how to build interactive web applications using Dart, including event handling, DOM manipulation, and client-side routing.

Event Handling and DOM Manipulation

Dart makes event handling and DOM manipulation straightforward. You can easily attach event listeners to HTML elements and respond to user interactions. Here's a basic example of handling a button click event:

```
import 'dart:html';

void main() {

var button = querySelector('#myButton');

button.onClick.listen((MouseEvent event) {

// Handle button click here

print('Button clicked!');

});

}
```

In this code, we select a button element with the ID "myButton" and attach a click event listener to it. When the button is clicked, the listener function is executed.

Dart also provides convenient methods for manipulating the DOM. You can add, remove, and modify HTML elements and their attributes easily. For instance, you can change the text content of a paragraph element like this:

```
import 'dart:html';

void main() {

var paragraph = querySelector('#myParagraph');

paragraph.text = 'New text content';

}
```

Clicnt-Side Routing

Client-side routing is a fundamental feature for single-page applications (SPAs) that provide a smoother user experience by updating the URL without causing a full page reload. Dart offers the route package for managing client-side routing in web applications.

To use the route package, you first need to include it in your project's pubspec.yaml file:

```
dependencies:

route: ^2.0.0
```

Then, you can define routes and handle route changes in your Dart code:

```
import 'package:route/client.dart';

void main() {

var router = Router();
```

```
router.root.addRoute(
name: 'home',
path: '/',
enter: (RouteEvent event) {
// Handle the home route
print('Home route activated');
},
);
router.root.addRoute(
name: 'about',
path: '/about',
enter: (RouteEvent event) {
// Handle the about route
print('About route activated');
},
);
router.listen();
}
```

In this example, we define two routes: "home" and "about." When the user navigates to these routes, the corresponding enter functions are executed.

Web Components

Web components are a set of web platform APIs that allow you to create custom, reusable HTML elements with encapsulated behavior and styling. Dart has built-in support for web components, making it easy to create your own custom elements.

Here's an example of defining a custom web component using Dart:

```
@HtmlImport('my_element.html')

library my_element;

import 'package:polymer/polymer.dart';

@PolymerRegister('my-element')

class MyElement extends PolymerElement {

@property String message = 'Hello, Dart!';

MyElement.created() : super.created();

}
```

In this code, we define a custom element "my-element" using the @PolymerRegister annotation. The element has a property "message" that can be used for data binding. The associated HTML template is defined in a separate file named "my_element.html."

State Management

Managing application state is crucial for building interactive web applications. Dart provides various state management solutions, including libraries like redux.dart and mobx.dart, to help you manage and update the state of your application efficiently.

State management libraries allow you to organize your application's data and ensure that changes in state trigger updates to the user interface, providing a smooth and responsive user experience.

Building interactive web applications with Dart is made accessible by its event handling capabilities, DOM manipulation tools, client-side routing support, and web component integration. Whether you're creating a single-page application or adding interactivity to a traditional web page, Dart's features and libraries can help you build dynamic and engaging user interfaces.

4.5 Dart in the World of Web Frameworks

Dart has established a presence in the world of web development through the development of various web frameworks and libraries that simplify web application development. In this section, we'll explore some of the notable web frameworks and libraries in the Dart ecosystem.

AngularDart

AngularDart is a port of the popular Angular framework to Dart. It offers a powerful and opinionated framework for building web applications. AngularDart follows the principles of component-based development and provides tools for creating complex user interfaces with a clear structure.

Here's a simple example of using AngularDart to create a component:

```
import 'package:angular/angular.dart';

@Component(

selector: 'my-app',
```

```
template: '<h1>Hello, {{name}}!</h1>',

)

class AppComponent {

String name = 'Dart';

}

void main() {

runApp(ng.AppComponentNgFactory);

}
```

In this code, we define an AngularDart component, AppComponent, with a template that displays a greeting. The component is then bootstrapped in the main function using runApp.

Flutter for Web

Flutter, originally designed for mobile app development, has extended its reach to the web with Flutter for Web. This framework allows you to build web applications using the same codebase as your mobile apps, enabling code sharing and a consistent user experience across platforms.

With Flutter for Web, you can create web applications that are visually appealing and performant. Flutter's rich widget library, hot-reloading for fast development, and support for Material Design make it an attractive choice for web development.

Here's a simple Flutter for Web example:

```
import 'package:flutter/material.dart';
```

```
void main() {
runApp(MyApp());
}
class MyApp extends StatelessWidget {
@override
Widget build(BuildContext context) {
return MaterialApp(
home: Scaffold(
appBar: AppBar(
title: Text('Flutter for Web Example'),
),
body: Center(
child: Text('Hello, Flutter for Web!'),
),
),
);
}
}
```

In this code, we create a basic Flutter for Web application that displays a simple message.

Shelf

Shelf is a minimalistic web framework for Dart that focuses on simplicity and extensibility. It provides the core components needed to build web applications, such as handling HTTP requests and responses, middleware support, and routing.

Shelf allows developers to build custom web applications tailored to their specific needs without imposing a rigid structure. It's particularly suitable for small to medium-sized projects and RESTful APIs.

Here's a basic example of using Shelf to create a simple web server:

```
import 'dart:io';

import 'package:shelf/shelf.dart';

import 'package:shelf/shelf_io.dart' as io;

void main() async {

var handler = const Pipeline()

.addMiddleware(logRequests())

.addHandler(_echoRequest);

var server = await io.serve(handler, 'localhost', 8080);

print('Server listening on ${server.address.host}:${server.port}');

}

Response _echoRequest(Request request) {

return Response.ok('Request for ${request.url}');
```

```
}
```

In this code, we create a basic web server using Shelf that listens on localhost port 8080 and responds with the requested URL.

Aqueduct

Aqueduct is a Dart framework for building scalable and RESTful web applications. It focuses on providing a structured architecture for creating APIs, database integration, and authentication. Aqueduct follows the principles of the Model-View-Controller (MVC) design pattern.

With Aqueduct, you can quickly build powerful and secure back-end services for your web applications. It includes features like automatic documentation generation, database migrations, and support for real-time applications.

Here's a simplified example of defining an Aqueduct application:

```
import 'package:aqueduct/aqueduct.dart';

class MyAppChannel extends ApplicationChannel {

@override

Future prepare() async {

logger.onRecord.listen((rec) => print('$rec ${rec.error ?? ''} ${rec.stackTrace ?? ''}'));

}

@override

Controller get entryPoint {
```

```
final router = Router();

router.route('/hello').linkFunction((request) async {

return Response.ok('Hello, Aqueduct!');

});

return router;

}

}

Future main() async {

final app = Application<MyAppChannel>()

..options.configurationFilePath = 'config.yaml'

..options.port = 8888;

await app.start(numberOfInstances: 3);

print('Server started on port ${app.options.port}.');

}
```

In this code, we define an Aqueduct application with a single route that responds with a greeting when accessed.

These are just a few examples of the web frameworks and libraries available in the Dart ecosystem. Depending on your project's requirements and your familiarity with a particular framework, you can choose the one that best suits your needs for web development in Dart. Each framework brings its unique features and advantages to the table, making Dart a versatile choice for web application development.

Chapter 5: Mobile App Development with Flutter

5.1 Flutter: The Future of Mobile Development

Flutter is a cross-platform framework developed by Google for building natively compiled applications for mobile, web, and desktop from a single codebase. It has gained significant popularity in the mobile app development world due to its efficiency, performance, and a wide range of customizable widgets. In this section, we'll explore why Flutter is considered the future of mobile app development.

Fast Development with Hot Reload

One of the standout features of Flutter is "Hot Reload." It allows developers to see the effects of code changes almost instantly in the running app, without the need for a full recompile and restart. This feature significantly speeds up the development process and enhances productivity. Developers can iterate quickly, experiment with UI changes, and fix issues in real-time, making development more enjoyable.

Here's an example of using Hot Reload in Flutter:

```
import 'package:flutter/material.dart';

void main() {

runApp(MyApp());

}
```

```
class MyApp extends StatelessWidget {

@override

Widget build(BuildContext context) {

return MaterialApp(

home: Scaffold(

appBar: AppBar(

title: Text('Hot Reload Example'),

),

body: Center(

child: Text('Hello, Flutter!'),

),

),

);

}

}
```

You can make changes to the text or UI in the build method, save the file, and see the updates instantly in the running app.

Single Codebase, Multiple Platforms

Flutter's core principle is "write once, run anywhere." With a single codebase, you can target multiple platforms, including iOS, Android, web, and desktop. This approach reduces development effort, maintenance costs, and ensures feature parity across platforms.

Flutter's widget-based architecture enables you to create custom UI elements that adapt to each platform's design guidelines seamlessly. It provides a consistent user experience while allowing you to fine-tune the UI for each platform if needed.

Rich Set of Customizable Widgets

Flutter comes with an extensive library of pre-designed widgets that you can use to create sophisticated user interfaces. These widgets are highly customizable, allowing you to match your app's design precisely to your vision.

Here are a few examples of Flutter widgets:

- Text: For displaying text with various styles.
- Button: For creating buttons with custom designs.
- ListView: For creating scrollable lists of items.
- TextField: For accepting user input.
- AppBar: For top app bars with titles and actions.

Flutter's widget system promotes a widget-first architecture, making it easy to create complex UIs by composing smaller, reusable widgets.

High Performance

Flutter apps are natively compiled, which means they run directly on the device's hardware without relying on a web view or an interpreter. This results in high-performance applications with smooth animations and fast rendering, providing an excellent user experience.

Flutter also includes a rendering engine called Skia, which is used for graphics and text rendering. Skia ensures that Flutter apps have a consistent look and feel across different platforms and screen sizes.

Strong Community and Ecosystem

Flutter has a vibrant and growing community of developers and a rich ecosystem of packages and plugins. You can find packages for various functionalities, such as accessing device features, working with APIs, and implementing complex UI elements. This extensive ecosystem accelerates development and simplifies integration with third-party services.

In conclusion, Flutter's combination of fast development with Hot Reload, cross-platform capabilities, customizable widgets, high performance, and a strong community make it a compelling choice for mobile app development. Its future looks promising, with continuous updates and improvements, positioning it as a frontrunner in the mobile development landscape. Whether you are a beginner or an experienced developer, Flutter provides a modern and efficient way to build mobile apps that stand out in terms of both functionality and design.

5.2 Setting Up a Flutter Environment

Before you start developing mobile apps with Flutter, you need to set up your development environment. Flutter supports multiple operating systems, including Windows, macOS, and Linux. In this section, we'll walk you through the steps to set up Flutter on your system.

Prerequisites

To get started with Flutter, you'll need the following prerequisites:

1. **Operating System**: Flutter supports Windows, macOS, and Linux. Ensure that you have a compatible operating system.
2. **Disk Space**: You'll need around 2GB of free disk space for the Flutter SDK and development tools.
3. **Git**: Git is required for fetching Flutter and Dart dependencies.
4. **IDE**: You can use various Integrated Development Environments (IDEs) for Flutter development, such as Android Studio, Visual Studio Code (VS Code), or IntelliJ IDEA. Choose the one that suits your preference.

Installing Flutter

Follow these steps to install Flutter on your system:

1. **Download the Flutter SDK**: Visit the Flutter download page and download the Flutter SDK for your operating system.
2. **Extract the Archive**: Once downloaded, extract the contents of the archive to a location on your system. For example, on macOS or Linux, you can use the following commands in the terminal:

```
tar xf flutter_linux_2.5.0-stable.tar.xz

mv flutter /usr/local/
```

Adjust the paths and filenames according to your downloaded archive.

1. **Add Flutter to Your Path**: To access Flutter commands globally, add the flutter/bin directory to your system's PATH. You can do this by modifying your shell's profile file (e.g., ~/.bashrc or ~/.zshrc) and adding the following line:

export PATH="$PATH:`pwd`/flutter/bin"

Save the file and run source ~/.bashrc (or the appropriate command for your shell) to apply the changes.

1. **Verify Installation**: Open a terminal and run the following command to verify that Flutter is correctly installed:

flutter—version

You should see output indicating the Flutter version and Dart version.

Installing Dart

Flutter uses the Dart programming language, so you'll also need to ensure Dart is installed on your system:

1. **Download the Dart SDK**: Visit the Dart download page and download the Dart SDK for your operating system.
2. **Extract and Install Dart**: Similar to the Flutter installation, extract the Dart SDK archive and move it to a suitable location on your system. Make sure to add the Dart SDK's bin directory to your system's PATH, just like you did with Flutter.
3. **Verify Dart Installation**: Open a terminal and run the following command to verify that Dart is correctly

installed:

dart—version

You should see output indicating the Dart version.

Configuring Your IDE

If you're using an IDE for Flutter development (e.g., Android Studio, VS Code, IntelliJ IDEA), you may need to install Flutter and Dart plugins or extensions. These plugins provide features like code completion, debugging, and project setup tailored for Flutter development.

Follow the official documentation for your chosen IDE to set up Flutter and Dart support.

Android and iOS Setup

To develop Flutter apps for Android and iOS, you'll also need to set up the necessary platform-specific tools and emulators. The official Flutter documentation provides detailed instructions for setting up your Android and iOS development environments.

- Setting up Flutter for Android development
- Setting up Flutter for iOS development

With Flutter, you can develop and test your mobile apps on emulators or physical devices for both Android and iOS, streamlining the development process.

Once you've completed these setup steps, you'll be ready to start building mobile apps with Flutter on your preferred development environment. The Flutter ecosystem offers an array of tools, libraries, and resources to help you create beautiful and performant cross-platform applications for mobile, web, and beyond.

5.3 Basics of Flutter Development with Dart

In this section, we will dive into the basics of Flutter development using the Dart programming language. Flutter allows you to build natively compiled applications for various platforms, with a primary focus on mobile (iOS and Android) while also enabling web and desktop development. Dart, as the language of choice for Flutter, offers a concise and expressive syntax, making it suitable for both beginners and experienced developers.

Creating Your First Flutter App

To get started with Flutter, you'll typically use a command-line tool called flutter. Here are the steps to create your first Flutter app:

1. **Create a New Flutter Project**:

   Open a terminal and run the following command to create a new Flutter project:

   flutter create my_first_flutter_app

   Replace "my_first_flutter_app" with the desired name for your project.

1. **Navigate to the Project Directory**:

   Change your working directory to the newly created project folder:

   cd my_first_flutter_app

1. **Open Your Project in an IDE**:

   You can open the project in your preferred Integrated Development Environment (IDE) such as Android Studio, Visual Studio Code, or IntelliJ IDEA. These IDEs offer Flutter and Dart plugins/extensions that streamline development.

1. **Run Your App**:

   To launch your app on an emulator or connected device, run the following command:

   ```
   flutter run
   ```

   This command will compile your code, start the Flutter development server, and launch your app on the selected device.

Understanding Flutter Widgets

Flutter uses a widget-based approach to building user interfaces. Everything in Flutter is a widget, from the app itself to the individual UI components. Widgets are either StatelessWidget or StatefulWidget, depending on whether they are static or have mutable state.

Here's an example of a simple Flutter widget:

```
import 'package:flutter/material.dart';

void main() {

runApp(MyApp());

}
```

```
class MyApp extends StatelessWidget {
@override
Widget build(BuildContext context) {
return MaterialApp(
home: Scaffold(
appBar: AppBar(
title: Text('My First Flutter App'),
),
body: Center(
child: Text('Hello, Flutter!'),
),
),
);
}
}
```

In this code, MyApp is a StatelessWidget that returns a MaterialApp widget, which sets up the app's basic structure. Inside MaterialApp, we have a Scaffold widget, which provides a standard app layout with an AppBar and a body. The body contains a Center widget, which centers its child, a Text widget displaying "Hello, Flutter!".

Stateful Widgets and Interactivity

When your app needs to handle user interactions or maintain mutable state, you can use StatefulWidget. Here's a simple example of a StatefulWidget:

```
import 'package:flutter/material.dart';

void main() {

runApp(MyApp());

}

class CounterApp extends StatefulWidget {

@override

_CounterAppState createState() => _CounterAppState();

}

class _CounterAppState extends State<CounterApp> {

int _counter = 0;

void _incrementCounter() {

setState(() {

_counter++;

});

}

@override

Widget build(BuildContext context) {
```

```
return MaterialApp(
home: Scaffold(
appBar: AppBar(
title: Text('Counter App'),
),
body: Center(
child: Column(
mainAxisAlignment: MainAxisAlignment.center,
children: <Widget>[
Text(
'Counter:',
style: TextStyle(fontSize: 24),
),
Text(
'$_counter',
style: TextStyle(fontSize: 48),
),
],
),
),
```

```
floatingActionButton: FloatingActionButton(
onPressed: _incrementCounter,
tooltip: 'Increment',
child: Icon(Icons.add),
),
),
);
}
}
```

In this code, CounterApp is a StatefulWidget that maintains the _counter state. The _incrementCounter function updates the counter and triggers a rebuild of the widget using setState. The UI is updated automatically to reflect the current counter value.

Flutter's Rich Ecosystem

Flutter offers a vast ecosystem of widgets, libraries, and packages that simplify common tasks and accelerate development. You can find widgets for handling navigation, animations, forms, and more. Additionally, the Flutter community actively contributes packages that extend Flutter's capabilities, making it a versatile framework for various app development needs.

With this basic understanding of Flutter development and Dart, you're ready to explore the world of Flutter and start building your mobile apps. Whether you're creating a simple app or a complex application, Flutter provides the tools and flexibility to bring your ideas to life on multiple platforms.

5.4 Designing User Interfaces in Flutter

Designing user interfaces (UI) is a crucial aspect of mobile app development, and Flutter provides a rich set of tools and widgets to create visually appealing and functional UIs. In this section, we'll explore the fundamentals of designing user interfaces in Flutter.

Flutter's Widget System

Flutter's UI is built using a widget-based system. Everything in Flutter is a widget, from simple elements like text and buttons to complex layouts and animations. Widgets are composable and reusable, making it easy to create complex UIs by combining smaller widgets.

Widgets in Flutter can be categorized into two main types:

- **StatelessWidgets**: These are widgets that don't have mutable state and are generally used for static UI elements. Stateless widgets are immutable, and their properties are set when they are created.

- **StatefulWidgets**: These are widgets that can change over time, typically in response to user interactions or external data. Stateful widgets maintain mutable state that can be updated, and they rebuild when their state changes.

Building a Basic UI

Let's start by building a simple UI using Flutter. Here's an example of a basic Flutter app that displays a "Hello, Flutter!" message:

```
import 'package:flutter/material.dart';
```

```
void main() {
runApp(MyApp());
}
class MyApp extends StatelessWidget {
@override
Widget build(BuildContext context) {
return MaterialApp(
home: Scaffold(
appBar: AppBar(
title: Text('My First Flutter App'),
),
body: Center(
child: Text('Hello, Flutter!'),
),
),
);
}
}
```

In this code, we create a MyApp widget that extends StatelessWidget. The build method of MyApp returns a MaterialApp, which is the root of the app's widget hierarchy. Within MaterialApp, we define a

Scaffold with an AppBar and a body that contains a Text widget. The Text widget displays the "Hello, Flutter!" message.

Styling and Theming

Flutter allows you to style and theme your app to give it a consistent and visually appealing look. You can customize various aspects of your app's appearance, such as fonts, colors, and layouts.

Here's an example of applying a custom theme to your Flutter app:

```
import 'package:flutter/material.dart';

void main() {

runApp(MyApp());

}

class MyApp extends StatelessWidget {

@override

Widget build(BuildContext context) {

return MaterialApp(

theme: ThemeData(

primaryColor: Colors.blue,

accentColor: Colors.orange,

fontFamily: 'Roboto',

),

home: Scaffold(
```

```
appBar: AppBar(
title: Text('Themed Flutter App'),
),
body: Center(
child: Text(
'Hello, Flutter!',
style: TextStyle(
fontSize: 24,
fontWeight: FontWeight.bold,
),
),
),
),
);
}
}
```

In this example, we set a custom theme using ThemeData. We specify the primary color as blue, the accent color as orange, and the font family as "Roboto." Additionally, we apply custom styles to the Text widget by setting the font size and weight.

Layouts and Widgets

Flutter provides a wide range of layout widgets to arrange UI elements on the screen. Some commonly used layout widgets include:

- **Container**: A versatile widget for containing other widgets with options for decoration and alignment.
- **Column**: Arranges child widgets vertically in a single column.
- **Row**: Arranges child widgets horizontally in a single row.
- **Stack**: Overlaps child widgets, allowing them to be positioned relative to each other.
- **ListView**: Creates scrollable lists of widgets.
- **GridView**: Arranges child widgets in a grid layout.
- **Expanded**: Allows a widget to take up remaining space within its parent.

These layout widgets, along with others, can be combined and nested to create complex and responsive UIs.

Responsive UI Design

Flutter makes it easier to create responsive user interfaces that adapt to different screen sizes and orientations. You can use layout widgets like Expanded, Flexible, and media query information to design UIs that work well on various devices.

For example, you can create responsive layouts for different screen sizes by checking the device's screen width:

```
double screenWidth = MediaQuery.of(context).size.width;

if (screenWidth > 600) {

// Display a different layout for larger screens

} else {

// Display the default layout

}
```

This allows you to adjust the UI elements based on the available screen real estate.

In conclusion, Flutter provides a powerful and flexible framework for designing user interfaces that are not only visually appealing but also highly functional. With its widget-based system, styling options, layout widgets, and responsive design capabilities, Flutter empowers developers to create UIs that meet the needs of various mobile and desktop platforms. Whether you're building a simple app or a complex one, Flutter's UI capabilities make the development process efficient and enjoyable.

5.5 State Management in Flutter Apps

State management is a crucial aspect of Flutter app development, especially for apps with dynamic user interfaces and data-driven components. In this section, we will explore the fundamentals of state management in Flutter and various techniques for managing the state of your Flutter applications.

What is State in Flutter?

In Flutter, "state" refers to any data that can be read asynchronously and might change over time. State can be as simple as a boolean value indicating whether a button is pressed or as complex as the data fetched from an API.

There are two main types of state in Flutter:

1. **Local State**: This state is specific to a single widget and doesn't need to be shared with other widgets. Local state is managed using the State class in a StatefulWidget.
2. **Global State**: This state needs to be shared across multiple widgets or persisted throughout the app's lifecycle. Global state is typically managed using state management libraries and techniques.

Local State Management

Local state is managed within a single widget using the State class. When a widget's state changes, Flutter automatically rebuilds the widget, updating its appearance based on the new state.

Here's a simple example of local state management using a StatefulWidget:

```
import 'package:flutter/material.dart';

void main() {

runApp(MyApp());

}

class CounterApp extends StatefulWidget {
```

```
@override
_CounterAppState createState() => _CounterAppState();
}
class _CounterAppState extends State<CounterApp> {
int _counter = 0;
void _incrementCounter() {
setState(() {
_counter++;
});
}
@override
Widget build(BuildContext context) {
return MaterialApp(
home: Scaffold(
appBar: AppBar(
title: Text('Counter App'),
),
body: Center(
child: Column(
mainAxisAlignment: MainAxisAlignment.center,
```

```
children: <Widget>[
Text(
'Counter:',
style: TextStyle(fontSize: 24),
),
Text(
'$_counter',
style: TextStyle(fontSize: 48),
),
],
),
),
floatingActionButton: FloatingActionButton(
onPressed: _incrementCounter,
tooltip: 'Increment',
child: Icon(Icons.add),
),
),
);
}
```

}

In this example, _counter is local state, and it's updated using the _incrementCounter function within the setState method. When _counter changes, the UI is automatically updated to reflect the new value.

Global State Management

Managing global state involves sharing data between multiple widgets or persisting data throughout the app's lifecycle. Flutter provides several options for global state management:

1. **InheritedWidget**: Flutter's built-in mechanism for passing data down the widget tree. It's suitable for small to medium-sized apps but can become complex for large apps.
2. **Provider Package**: A popular third-party package that simplifies state management using the Provider pattern. It's efficient and works well for many use cases.
3. **Redux**: A state management library inspired by Redux, commonly used for larger apps with complex state needs. It enforces a unidirectional data flow.
4. **BLoC (Business Logic Component)**: A pattern and library for handling state management and reactive programming in Flutter. It's suitable for apps with a heavy focus on streams and events.
5. **GetX**: Another third-party package that offers state management, dependency injection, and routing, making it a comprehensive solution for Flutter apps.

The choice of state management technique depends on the complexity and specific requirements of your app. Smaller apps may benefit from simpler solutions like InheritedWidget or Provider, while larger apps with complex state interactions may require Redux, BLoC, or GetX.

In conclusion, state management is a critical aspect of Flutter app development, allowing you to create dynamic and responsive user interfaces. Understanding the difference between local and global state and choosing the appropriate state management technique for your app's needs is essential for building maintainable and efficient Flutter applications.

Chapter 6: Dart and Databases

6.1 Introduction to Databases in Dart

Databases play a pivotal role in modern software development, enabling the storage, retrieval, and management of data efficiently. Dart, being a versatile programming language, offers various options for working with databases. In this section, we will explore the fundamentals of databases in Dart, the types of databases available, and how to interact with them in your Dart applications.

What is a Database?

A database is a structured collection of data that is organized, stored, and managed in a way that allows for efficient retrieval and manipulation. Databases are used to store a wide range of information, from simple user profiles to complex financial records and multimedia content.

Types of Databases

There are primarily two types of databases: relational databases (SQL databases) and non-relational databases (NoSQL databases). Each type has its own strengths and is suitable for specific use cases:

1. Relational Databases (SQL):

- Structure: Data is organized into tables with predefined schemas.
- Query Language: SQL (Structured Query Language) is used for querying and manipulating data.
- Use Cases: Well-suited for applications with complex relationships between data entities, such as financial systems and e-commerce platforms.

2. Non-relational Databases (NoSQL):

- Structure: Data can be stored in various formats, including JSON, XML, or key-value pairs.
- Query Language: NoSQL databases often use flexible query languages or APIs for data retrieval.
- Use Cases: Ideal for handling unstructured or semi-structured data, making them popular in web and mobile applications.

Dart and Databases

Dart provides libraries and packages that make it relatively straightforward to work with both SQL and NoSQL databases. You can choose a database solution based on your project requirements and preferences. Here are some commonly used databases and Dart libraries for each type:

SQL Databases:

- **sqflite**: A popular Dart package for working with SQLite, a lightweight and embedded SQL database.
- **moor**: An efficient and type-safe way to work with SQLite databases in Dart, offering a fluent query API.

NoSQL Databases:

- **mongo_dart**: A Dart package for MongoDB, a NoSQL database known for its flexibility and scalability.
- **firebase**: Firebase, a popular mobile and web application development platform, offers real-time NoSQL database support for Dart apps.

In the next sections of this chapter, we will delve deeper into working with SQL and NoSQL databases in Dart, including database setup, data modeling, CRUD operations, and advanced database techniques. Whether you are building a web application, mobile app, or server-side application, understanding how to work with databases in Dart is essential for creating data-driven and efficient applications.

6.2 Working with SQL Databases

In this section, we will focus on working with SQL databases in Dart. SQL databases are widely used for structured data storage and retrieval. Dart provides several libraries and packages that make it relatively easy to work with SQL databases, with SQLite being one of the most popular choices. We will cover the following topics:

SQLite in Dart

SQLite is a lightweight, serverless, and self-contained SQL database engine used extensively in mobile and desktop applications. Dart provides the sqflite package, which allows you to work with SQLite databases efficiently. You can use sqflite for tasks such as creating, querying, and updating SQLite databases in your Dart applications.

Installing sqflite

To get started with sqflite, you need to add it to your Dart project's dependencies. You can do this by adding the following lines to your pubspec.yaml file:

dependencies:

sqflite: ^2.0.0

After adding the dependency, run pub get or flutter pub get to fetch and install the package.

Creating a SQLite Database

Once you have sqflite installed, you can create a new SQLite database in your Dart application. To do this, you typically perform the following steps:

1. Open a database connection to a file or in-memory database.
2. Define the database schema by creating tables and specifying their columns and data types.

3. Perform CRUD (Create, Read, Update, Delete) operations on the database.

Here's a basic example of how to create a SQLite database and define a table using sqflite:

```
import 'package:sqflite/sqflite.dart';

void main() async {

final database = openDatabase(

// Provide the path to the database file

'my_database.db',

version: 1,

onCreate: (db, version) {

// Create a table when the database is first created

return db.execute(

'CREATE TABLE users(id INTEGER PRIMARY KEY, name TEXT, email TEXT)',

);

},

);

// Wait for the database to be opened

final db = await database;

// Perform database operations here
```

}

In this example, we open a database connection to a file named my_database.db and specify the database schema by creating a users table with columns for id, name, and email. The onCreate callback is called when the database is first created.

Performing Database Operations

Once you have a SQLite database set up, you can perform various database operations, including inserting, querying, updating, and deleting records. sqflite provides a fluent API for executing SQL statements and working with the database.

Here's a brief overview of some common database operations:

Inserting Data

To insert data into a SQLite database, you can use the insert method:

await db.insert('users', {'name': 'Alice', 'email': 'alice@example.com'});

Querying Data

To retrieve data from the database, you can use the query method:

final users = await db.query('users');

for (final user in users) {

print('User: ${user['name']}, Email: ${user['email']}');

}

Updating Data

To update existing records, use the update method:

```
await db.update(

'users',

{'name': 'Alice Updated'},

where: 'name = ?',

whereArgs: ['Alice'],

);
```

Deleting Data

To delete records from the database, use the delete method:

```
await db.delete('users', where: 'name = ?', whereArgs: ['Alice Updated']);
```

Error Handling and Transactions

When working with databases, it's important to handle errors and use transactions when performing multiple database operations to maintain data integrity. sqflite provides mechanisms for handling errors and using transactions to ensure consistency in your database operations.

In summary, working with SQL databases in Dart using sqflite involves creating a database, defining tables, and performing CRUD operations. Understanding how to interact with SQL databases is essential for building data-driven Dart applications.

6.3 NoSQL Databases: An Overview

In this section, we'll explore NoSQL databases in the context of Dart. NoSQL databases have gained popularity due to their flexibility and scalability, making them suitable for various types of applications. Dart developers can work with NoSQL databases using libraries like mongo_dart and by integrating with cloud-based NoSQL solutions like Firebase Firestore.

What Are NoSQL Databases?

NoSQL databases, as the name suggests, are databases that do not rely on the traditional SQL (Structured Query Language) for data storage and retrieval. They are designed to handle a wide variety of data types and are particularly well-suited for scenarios where data structures may evolve over time or where high scalability is required.

NoSQL databases can be classified into several categories based on their data models:

1. **Document Stores:** These databases store data in semi-structured documents, typically in formats like JSON or BSON (Binary JSON). Each document can have its own unique structure, making them flexible for storing different types of data. Examples include MongoDB and Firebase Firestore.
2. **Key-Value Stores:** Key-value stores associate a unique key with a data value, allowing efficient retrieval of data by its key. These databases are simple and fast but may not provide advanced querying capabilities. Examples include Redis and Riak.
3. **Column-Family Stores:** These databases store data in column families, where each column family contains multiple rows with varying columns. They are often used

for time-series data or data with sparse attributes. Apache Cassandra is an example of a column-family store.

4. **Graph Databases:** Graph databases are designed for managing highly interconnected data, such as social networks or recommendation systems. They represent data as nodes and edges in a graph structure. Examples include Neo4j and Amazon Neptune.

NoSQL Databases in Dart

Dart provides libraries like mongo_dart that enable developers to work with NoSQL databases, specifically MongoDB. MongoDB is a popular document-oriented NoSQL database that stores data in BSON format (Binary JSON). With mongo_dart, you can connect to a MongoDB database, perform CRUD operations, and interact with data in Dart applications.

Working with mongo_dart

To use mongo_dart, you need to add it to your Dart project's dependencies by including the following lines in your pubspec.yaml file:

```
dependencies:

mongo_dart: ^latest_version
```

After adding the dependency, run pub get or flutter pub get to install the package.

Here's a basic example of how to connect to a MongoDB database and perform CRUD operations using mongo_dart:

```
import 'package:mongo_dart/mongo_dart.dart';
```

```
void main() async {

final db = Db('mongodb://localhost:27017/my_database');

await db.open();

// Create a collection

final collection = db.collection('users');

// Insert a document

await collection.insert({'name': 'Alice', 'email': 'alice@example.com'});

// Query documents

final users = await collection.find().toList();

for (final user in users) {

print('User: ${user['name']}, Email: ${user['email']}');

}

// Update a document

await collection.update(

where.eq('name', 'Alice'),

modify.set('name', 'Alice Updated'),

);

// Delete a document

await collection.remove(where.eq('name', 'Alice Updated'));

// Close the database connection
```

```
await db.close();

}
```

In this example, we connect to a MongoDB database, create a collection called users, insert and query documents, update a document, and then delete it. mongo_dart provides a convenient API for working with MongoDB in Dart applications.

Cloud-Based NoSQL Solutions

While mongo_dart allows you to work with self-hosted MongoDB databases, Dart developers can also leverage cloud-based NoSQL solutions like Firebase Firestore. Firestore offers a serverless, scalable NoSQL database with real-time synchronization, making it suitable for web and mobile applications.

To integrate Firestore with your Dart application, you can use the firebase package and Firebase SDKs. Firestore provides a document-oriented data model with support for queries, real-time updates, and offline persistence.

In summary, NoSQL databases offer flexibility and scalability for data storage in Dart applications. Developers can work with NoSQL databases using libraries like mongo_dart and integrate with cloud-based solutions like Firebase Firestore for a seamless development experience. Understanding the strengths and trade-offs of different NoSQL database types is essential for choosing the right one for your project.

6.4 Dart and Firebase: Real-Time Data Handling

In this section, we will explore how to work with Firebase, a popular cloud-based platform, in Dart applications. Firebase offers real-time database capabilities, among other features, which can be incredibly useful for building responsive and collaborative applications. We'll focus on Firebase Realtime Database and Firestore, two of Firebase's real-time data storage solutions.

Firebase Realtime Database

Firebase Realtime Database is a NoSQL cloud-hosted database that stores data in JSON format and allows real-time data synchronization across clients. Dart developers can interact with Firebase Realtime Database using the firebase_database package. Here's an overview of how to get started:

Setting Up Firebase

1. Create a Firebase project on the Firebase Console.
2. Add your Dart application to the Firebase project by registering it on the console and downloading the configuration file (google-services.json for Android or GoogleService-Info.plist for iOS).
3. Add the firebase_database package to your Dart project's dependencies in the pubspec.yaml file.

dependencies:

firebase_database: ^latest_version

1. Initialize Firebase in your Dart application using the Firebase configuration:

```
import 'package:firebase_core/firebase_core.dart';

void main() async {

WidgetsFlutterBinding.ensureInitialized();

await Firebase.initializeApp(

options: FirebaseOptions(

apiKey: 'your_api_key',

appId: 'your_app_id',

messagingSenderId: 'your_messaging_sender_id',

projectId: 'your_project_id',

databaseURL: 'your_database_url',

),

);

// Continue with your Dart application code

}
```

Real-Time Data Updates

Firebase Realtime Database enables real-time data synchronization between clients, making it ideal for applications that require live updates. Here's an example of how to read and write data in real-time using Dart and Firebase:

```
import 'package:firebase_database/firebase_database.dart';

void main() {
```

```
final database = FirebaseDatabase.instance.reference();

// Write data to the database

database.child('messages').push().set({

'text': 'Hello, Firebase!',

'timestamp': ServerValue.timestamp,

});

// Read data in real-time

database.child('messages').onChildAdded.listen((event) {

print('New message: ${event.snapshot.value['text']}');

});

}
```

In this example, we push a new message to the messages node in the database with a timestamp. Clients listening to the onChildAdded event will receive real-time updates whenever a new message is added.

Firebase Firestore

Firebase Firestore is another real-time NoSQL database offered by Firebase. It provides more advanced querying capabilities and supports larger datasets. Dart developers can interact with Firestore using the cloud_firestore package. Here's an overview of how to get started:

Setting Up Firebase

1. Create a Firebase project on the Firebase Console.
2. Add your Dart application to the Firebase project by registering it on the console and downloading the configuration file (google-services.json for Android or GoogleService-Info.plist for iOS).
3. Add the cloud_firestore package to your Dart project's dependencies in the pubspec.yaml file.

```
dependencies:

cloud_firestore: ^latest_version
```

1. Initialize Firebase in your Dart application using the Firebase configuration, as shown in the previous section.

Querying Firestore

Firestore offers more complex querying capabilities compared to Firebase Realtime Database. Here's an example of how to query data from Firestore in a Dart application:

```
import 'package:cloud_firestore/cloud_firestore.dart';

void main() async {

final firestore = FirebaseFirestore.instance;

// Query documents

final querySnapshot = await firestore.collection('posts').where('likes', isGreaterThan: 100).get();

// Print matching documents
```

```
for (final document in querySnapshot.docs) {

print('Post Title: ${document.data()['title']}');

}

}
```

In this example, we query documents from a posts collection where the likes field is greater than 100. Firestore's flexible querying makes it suitable for various data retrieval scenarios.

Choosing Between Firebase Realtime Database and Firestore

When deciding between Firebase Realtime Database and Firestore for your Dart application, consider the following factors:

- **Data Structure:** Firebase Realtime Database is JSON-based and more suitable for simpler data structures, while Firestore offers more structured data with collections and documents.

- **Querying:** Firestore provides more powerful querying capabilities, including compound queries and indexing, making it better for complex data queries.

- **Scalability:** Firestore is designed to handle larger datasets and scales better for applications with high read/write rates.

- **Real-Time Updates:** Both databases support real-time updates, but Firestore offers more control over how data is synchronized.

In summary, Firebase Realtime Database and Firestore are valuable tools for real-time data handling in Dart applications. The choice between them depends on your project's specific requirements and data structure.

6.5 Effective Data Persistence Strategies

In this section, we will discuss effective data persistence strategies for Dart applications. Data persistence is a crucial aspect of application development, as it ensures that data is preserved even when the application is closed or the device is restarted. Dart offers various methods for data persistence, including local storage, databases, and cloud-based solutions. Choosing the right strategy depends on the nature of your application and its requirements.

Local Storage

Local storage refers to the ability to store data on the user's device. Dart provides the shared_preferences package for simple key-value storage, which is suitable for storing small amounts of data such as user preferences and settings. Here's an example of using shared_preferences:

```
import 'package:shared_preferences/shared_preferences.dart';

void main() async {

final prefs = await SharedPreferences.getInstance();

// Saving data

prefs.setString('username', 'Alice');

prefs.setInt('age', 30);

// Retrieving data
```

```
final username = prefs.getString('username');

final age = prefs.getInt('age');

print('Username: $username, Age: $age');

}
```

While shared_preferences is convenient for small data, it's not suitable for large datasets or structured data.

SQLite Databases

For more extensive data storage and structured data, you can use SQLite databases in Dart. The sqflite package allows you to create and interact with SQLite databases. Here's an example:

```
import 'package:sqflite/sqflite.dart';

void main() async {

final database = await openDatabase('my_database.db', version: 1,

onCreate: (Database db, int version) async {

await db.execute(

'CREATE TABLE users (id INTEGER PRIMARY KEY, name TEXT, age INTEGER)');

});

// Insert data

await database.rawInsert(

'INSERT INTO users(name, age) VALUES (?, ?)', ['Alice', 30]);

// Query data
```

```
final result = await database.rawQuery('SELECT * FROM users');

print(result);

// Close the database

await database.close();

}
```

SQLite databases are suitable for complex data structures and larger datasets, making them a good choice for applications that require robust data persistence.

Cloud-Based Solutions

For cloud-based data persistence, Firebase Firestore and Firebase Realtime Database, as discussed in the previous sections, offer real-time synchronization of data across devices. They are suitable for applications that need data to be accessible from multiple platforms and require real-time updates.

When choosing a data persistence strategy, consider factors like data size, complexity, offline access requirements, and the need for real-time updates. Combining different strategies, such as using local storage for settings and SQLite databases for structured data, can provide a comprehensive solution for data persistence in your Dart application.

Remember to handle data securely, especially when dealing with sensitive information, and to implement data backup and recovery mechanisms to prevent data loss in case of unexpected events. Effective data persistence is essential for delivering a seamless and reliable user experience in your Dart applications.

7.1 Writing Testable Code in Dart

In this section, we will explore the importance of writing testable code in Dart applications and discuss various testing techniques and best practices. Writing testable code is a fundamental aspect of software development that contributes to code quality, reliability, and maintainability.

The Importance of Testable Code

Testable code refers to code that is designed in a way that makes it easy to write automated tests. These tests, often referred to as unit tests or integration tests, help ensure that your code behaves as expected and continues to work correctly as it evolves. Here are some reasons why writing testable code is crucial:

1. Quality Assurance

Automated tests act as a safety net for your code, catching bugs and regressions early in the development process. This helps maintain code quality and prevents the introduction of new issues.

2. Code Confidence

Having a comprehensive test suite gives you confidence in your code's correctness. You can make changes or refactor code with the assurance that existing functionality won't break unnoticed.

3. Collaboration

Testable code facilitates collaboration among team members. Tests serve as documentation, providing insights into how components are expected to behave.

4. Maintainability

Testable code tends to be more modular and follows best practices, making it easier to maintain and extend. It promotes cleaner code architecture and separation of concerns.

Writing Testable Dart Code

To write testable Dart code, consider the following principles and techniques:

1. Separation of Concerns

Adhering to the principle of separation of concerns (SoC) helps in writing testable code. Separate your code into distinct modules, each responsible for a specific aspect of functionality. This separation makes it easier to test individual units of code in isolation.

2. Dependency Injection

Use dependency injection to provide dependencies, such as services and data sources, to your classes. This allows you to substitute real dependencies with mock objects or stubs during testing. The provider package and Dart's built-in dependency injection support can be helpful in this regard.

3. Mocking and Stubbing

In unit tests, replace external dependencies with mock objects or stubs. Libraries like mockito provide useful tools for creating mock objects and specifying their behavior during testing.

4. Immutability

Immutable data structures simplify testing since they have predictable and consistent behavior. Dart's support for immutable data structures, such as lists and maps, can help in writing more testable code.

5. Test-Driven Development (TDD)

Consider adopting Test-Driven Development (TDD) practices. In TDD, you write tests before implementing the actual code. This ensures that the code is designed to be testable from the start.

6. Code Coverage

Monitor code coverage to ensure that your tests exercise a significant portion of your codebase. Tools like the coverage package can help you measure code coverage and identify areas that need more testing.

7. Continuous Integration

Integrate automated tests into your continuous integration (CI) pipeline. CI systems like Travis CI, CircleCI, or GitHub Actions can run tests automatically whenever changes are pushed to your code repository.

8. Use Testing Frameworks

Leverage testing frameworks like flutter_test for Flutter applications and test for Dart applications. These frameworks provide essential tools for writing and running tests.

Let's look at a simple example of writing a unit test for a Dart function:

```
// Code to be tested
```

```
int add(int a, int b) {
return a + b;
}
// Unit test
void main() {
test('Addition test', () {
expect(add(2, 3), 5); // Verify that add(2, 3) returns 5
});
}
```

In this example, we write a unit test using the test function provided by the test package. The expect function checks if the result of the add function matches the expected value.

Conclusion

Writing testable code is a critical skill for Dart developers. It ensures the reliability and maintainability of your applications. By following best practices and using testing frameworks and tools, you can create a robust test suite that helps you build high-quality Dart applications.

7.2 Unit Testing and Integration Testing

In this section, we delve into the world of testing in Dart, focusing on both unit testing and integration testing. Testing is an integral part of software development, ensuring that your code works as expected and that changes or updates do not introduce regressions.

Unit Testing

Unit testing involves testing individual units or components of your code in isolation. These units are typically functions, methods, or classes. Unit tests are valuable for verifying that small, specific pieces of your code behave correctly. Dart provides a built-in testing framework called test that makes it easy to write and run unit tests.

To write a unit test in Dart, you use the test function from the test package, which provides a convenient way to define test cases and assertions. Here's an example of a simple unit test:

```
import 'package:test/test.dart';

int add(int a, int b) {

return a + b;

}

void main() {

test('Addition test', () {

expect(add(2, 3), 5); // Verify that add(2, 3) returns 5

});

}
```

In this example, we define a function add and write a unit test to ensure that it correctly adds two numbers. The expect function checks if the result of add(2, 3) is equal to 5.

Integration Testing

Integration testing goes beyond individual units and tests the interaction between different parts of your code. This type of testing is essential to ensure that different components of your application work together as expected. Dart provides tools for integration testing as well.

Flutter, a popular framework for building mobile applications with Dart, includes a robust testing framework for widget testing. Widget tests allow you to test the UI components of your Flutter application, including their interaction and behavior.

Here's an example of a simple Flutter widget test:

```
import 'package:flutter_test/flutter_test.dart';

import 'package:my_app/main.dart';

void main() {

testWidgets('Counter increments', (WidgetTester tester) async {

// Build our app and trigger a frame.

await tester.pumpWidget(MyApp());

// Verify that our counter starts at 0.

expect(find.text('0'), findsOneWidget);

expect(find.text('1'), findsNothing);

// Tap the '+' icon and trigger a frame.

await tester.tap(find.byIcon(Icons.add));

await tester.pump();
```

```
// Verify that our counter has incremented.

expect(find.text('0'), findsNothing);

expect(find.text('1'), findsOneWidget);

});

}
```

In this Flutter widget test, we test the behavior of a counter app by simulating user interactions, such as tapping a button. The test checks if the UI elements update correctly.

Test Driven Development (TDD)

Test Driven Development (TDD) is a development approach where you write tests before implementing the actual code. TDD ensures that your code is designed to be testable from the start and that it meets the desired functionality. Following TDD principles can lead to more reliable and maintainable code.

When practicing TDD, you start by writing a failing test case that describes the behavior you want to achieve. Then, you implement the code to make the test pass. Finally, you refactor the code while ensuring that the test still passes.

Continuous Integration (CI)

Integrating testing into your Continuous Integration (CI) pipeline is crucial for automating the testing process. CI systems like Travis CI, CircleCI, or GitHub Actions can automatically run your tests whenever changes are pushed to your code repository, providing quick feedback on the code's integrity.

In conclusion, both unit testing and integration testing are essential for ensuring the quality and reliability of your Dart applications. Whether you are writing pure Dart code or developing Flutter apps, incorporating testing into your development workflow is a best practice that leads to more robust and maintainable software.

7.3 Debugging Techniques in Dart

Debugging is a critical skill for developers, as it helps identify and fix issues in your code. Dart provides several debugging techniques and tools to aid in the debugging process, ensuring the smooth development of your applications.

1. Print Statements

The simplest debugging technique is to use print statements to output information to the console. You can insert print statements at various points in your code to inspect variable values, function calls, or control flow. For example:

```
void main() {

int a = 5;

int b = 7;

print('Before addition: a=$a, b=$b');

int result = a + b;

print('After addition: result=$result');

}
```

2. Debugger in IDEs

Modern Integrated Development Environments (IDEs) for Dart, like Visual Studio Code, IntelliJ IDEA, and Android Studio, come with built-in debuggers. These debuggers allow you to set breakpoints, inspect variables, and step through your code line by line, making it easier to pinpoint issues.

To use the debugger in an IDE, set breakpoints by clicking on the line numbers in your code. Then, run your Dart application in debug mode. The debugger will pause execution at breakpoints, allowing you to examine the state of your application.

3. Logging

Logging is an effective way to gather information about your application's behavior, especially in production environments where using print statements may not be suitable. Dart provides the logging package, which allows you to configure loggers and log messages with different log levels.

Here's an example of how to use the logging package:

```
import 'package:logging/logging.dart';

void main() {

Logger.root.level = Level.ALL;

Logger.root.onRecord.listen((record) {

print('${record.level.name}: ${record.time}: ${record.message}');

});

final logger = Logger('myApp');
```

```
logger.info('This is an info message.');

logger.warning('This is a warning message.');

logger.severe('This is a severe message.');

}
```

4. Dart DevTools

Dart DevTools is a powerful web-based tool that comes with the Dart SDK. It provides a graphical interface for debugging and profiling Dart applications. You can use it to inspect the widget tree in Flutter applications, view logs, examine performance profiles, and more.

To use Dart DevTools, run your Dart or Flutter application and navigate to http://localhost:8181 in your web browser. You can then connect to your running application and access various debugging features.

5. Remote Debugging

Dart also supports remote debugging, which allows you to debug applications running on remote devices or emulators. This can be particularly useful for debugging Flutter apps on mobile devices. You can use tools like flutter attach to connect to a running app on a physical device and debug it from your development environment.

6. Exception Handling

Properly handling exceptions is a crucial part of debugging. Dart provides try-catch blocks for catching and handling exceptions gracefully. When an exception occurs, you can use the catch block to log information or perform error recovery.

```
void main() {
try {
int result = 5 ~/ 0; // Division by zero will throw an exception
print('Result: $result'); // This line will not execute
} catch (e) {
print('An error occurred: $e'); // Handle the exception
}
}
```

In this example, when a division by zero exception occurs, the catch block is executed, preventing the application from crashing.

7. Testing and Test-Driven Development (TDD)

As mentioned in previous sections, writing unit tests and following Test-Driven Development practices can help catch and prevent bugs early in the development process. Writing tests that reproduce issues is an effective way to diagnose and fix problems.

In conclusion, debugging is an essential skill for Dart developers, and Dart provides various tools and techniques to make the process efficient. Whether you prefer using print statements, integrated debuggers, logging, or more advanced tools like Dart DevTools, understanding how to debug effectively is crucial for building reliable Dart applications.

7.4 Performance Tuning and Optimization

Performance tuning and optimization are essential aspects of software development, ensuring that your Dart applications run efficiently and provide a responsive user experience. In this section, we'll explore various techniques and best practices for improving the performance of your Dart applications.

1. Profiling Your Code

Before you can optimize your Dart code, you need to identify performance bottlenecks. Profiling tools, such as the Dart Observatory and Dart DevTools, can help you analyze the execution of your code and pinpoint areas that need improvement.

Dart Observatory is a web-based profiling tool that comes with the Dart SDK. It allows you to inspect CPU usage, memory allocation, and isolate-specific metrics. You can run it alongside your Dart application by adding the —observe flag when running your code. For example:

dart—observe my_app.dart

Dart DevTools also provides profiling capabilities, allowing you to analyze your Flutter application's performance. You can access it by running your Flutter app and navigating to http://localhost:8181 in your web browser.

2. Reduce Redundant Operations

One common source of performance issues is redundant or unnecessary operations. Analyze your code for repetitive calculations or data processing that can be optimized. Caching frequently used values and avoiding redundant work can lead to significant performance improvements.

```
// Inefficient code that computes the same result multiple times

for (int i = 0; i < items.length; i++) {

final item = items[i];

final result = expensiveOperation(item);

print(result);

}

// Optimized code using caching

for (int i = 0; i < items.length; i++) {

final item = items[i];

final result = cachedResults[item] ??= expensiveOperation(item);

print(result);

}
```

3. Use Efficient Data Structures

Choosing the right data structures can have a substantial impact on your application's performance. Dart provides a variety of built-in collections like lists, maps, and sets. Ensure that you select the appropriate data structure for your specific use case to minimize data retrieval and manipulation overhead.

```
// Inefficient use of List for item lookup

final List<Item> items = /* ... */;

final itemToFind = /* ... */;
```

```
final foundItem = items.firstWhere((item) => item.id == itemToFind.id);

// Optimized use of a Set for efficient lookup

final Set<Item> itemsSet = /* ... */;

final foundItem = itemsSet.firstWhere((item) => item.id == itemToFind.id, orElse: () => null);
```

4. Avoid Unnecessary Render Operations in Flutter

In Flutter, rendering is a critical aspect of performance. Minimize unnecessary rendering by using the const keyword where applicable, as it tells Flutter to reuse widgets when their properties do not change. Additionally, use the const constructor for custom widgets whenever possible.

```
// Without const keyword (potentially causes unnecessary rendering)

Container(

color: Colors.blue,

child: Text('Hello, Flutter!'),

)

// With const keyword (more efficient as it reuses widgets)

const Container(

color: Colors.blue,

child: Text('Hello, Flutter!'),

)
```

5. Optimize Network Requests

In applications that rely on network requests, optimizing network operations can significantly improve performance. Use techniques like caching, request batching, and optimizing payload sizes to reduce the load on the network and improve response times.

6. Memory Management

Efficient memory usage is crucial for performance. Avoid memory leaks by cleaning up resources when they are no longer needed. In Flutter, use the dispose method to release resources held by widgets and controllers.

```
class MyWidget extends StatefulWidget {

@override

_MyWidgetState createState() => _MyWidgetState();

}

class _MyWidgetState extends State<MyWidget> {

final _controller = TextEditingController();

@override

void dispose() {

_controller.dispose(); // Release resources

super.dispose();

}

// Widget build method...
```

```
}
```

7. Testing and Profiling

Regularly test your application's performance on various devices and screen sizes. Profiling on real hardware can uncover device-specific performance issues. Use tools like the Android Profiler and Xcode Instruments for mobile app profiling.

8. Lazy Loading

In cases where you have a large dataset or resource-heavy content, consider implementing lazy loading. This technique loads content only when it's needed, reducing initial load times and memory consumption.

Optimizing Dart applications for performance is an ongoing process. Continuously monitor and profile your code, implement performance improvements, and test on various devices to ensure a smooth and responsive user experience.

7.5 Continuous Integration and Delivery in Dart

Continuous Integration (CI) and Continuous Delivery (CD) are crucial practices in modern software development. They ensure that your Dart applications are built, tested, and deployed consistently and automatically, reducing the risk of bugs and streamlining the development process. In this section, we'll explore CI/CD concepts and how to implement them in Dart projects.

1. Continuous Integration (CI)

CI involves regularly integrating code changes into a shared repository, automatically building and testing them to catch issues early in the development cycle. Here are the key steps to set up CI for your Dart project:

Choose a CI Service:

Popular CI services for Dart projects include Travis CI, CircleCI, and GitHub Actions. Choose one that integrates well with your version control system (e.g., GitHub or GitLab).

Configuration File:

Create a configuration file (e.g., .travis.yml for Travis CI) in your project's root directory. This file defines the build environment, dependencies, and scripts for testing and building your Dart application.

```
language: dart

dart:

- stable

- beta

- dev

script:

- dart pub get

- dart test
```

Automatic Testing:

Set up automated testing using Dart's built-in testing framework or a testing library like flutter_test for Flutter projects. Ensure that your tests cover critical functionality and edge cases.

Push to Repository:

Commit and push your code changes to the repository. CI services will automatically detect the changes and trigger the build process.

Review Results:

Monitor the CI service for build results and test outcomes. If any issues arise, you'll receive notifications, allowing you to address them promptly.

2. Continuous Delivery (CD)

CD extends CI by automating the deployment of code changes to various environments (e.g., staging and production) after passing tests. Here's how to set up CD for your Dart project:

Deployment Scripts:

Create deployment scripts that specify how your Dart application should be deployed. These scripts might involve copying files to a server, configuring environment variables, or triggering a deployment pipeline.

```
#!/bin/bash

# Deploy script (example)
```

echo "Deploying Dart app to production..."

 # Copy files to the production server

 # Restart the server, if necessary

echo "Deployment completed."

Staging Environment:

Set up a staging environment that closely resembles your production environment. This allows you to test changes in a controlled environment before deploying to production.

Deployment Pipeline:

Create a deployment pipeline that automates the process of deploying code changes. CD services like Jenkins, GitLab CI/CD, or GitHub Actions can help with this.

 # Example GitHub Actions workflow for CD

name: Continuous Delivery

on:

push:

branches:

- main

jobs:

deploy:

runs-on: ubuntu-latest

steps:

- name: Checkout code

uses: actions/checkout@v2

- name: Deploy to production

run: ./deploy.sh

Automated Deployment:

After code changes pass CI tests, the CD pipeline will automatically deploy them to the specified environment (e.g., staging or production). This ensures that you consistently deliver reliable and tested updates to users.

3. Monitoring and Rollback

Implement monitoring and error tracking in your Dart application. If issues arise in the deployed version, you can quickly identify and roll back to a previous stable release. Services like Sentry and Rollbar can help with error tracking.

CI/CD practices significantly enhance the reliability and efficiency of Dart applications. By automating the build, test, and deployment processes, you can focus on improving your app's functionality and user experience while minimizing the risk of bugs in production.

8.1 Standard Libraries in Dart

Dart comes with a comprehensive set of standard libraries that provide essential functionality for a wide range of tasks. These libraries are available out-of-the-box and cover everything from basic data types to advanced features. In this section, we'll explore some of the key standard libraries in Dart and how you can leverage them in your Dart projects.

1. dart:core

The dart:core library is automatically imported into every Dart program and contains fundamental classes and functions. Here are some important components of this library:

- Object: The root class for all Dart objects. It defines methods like toString(), hashCode, and ==.

- int and double: Dart's integer and floating-point number types.

- String: The class for handling text data, with various methods for manipulation.

- List and Map: Collections for storing and manipulating data. Lists are ordered and allow duplicates, while maps store key-value pairs.

- Iterable and Iterator: Classes for working with sequences of data.

- DateTime: For working with dates and times.

- Exception: The base class for all exceptions in Dart.

- Function: Represents functions as objects.

2. dart:io

The dart:io library provides access to input and output operations, allowing you to work with files, directories, and network resources.

It's particularly useful for building command-line applications and server-side code. Here are some key classes and functions from this library:

- File and Directory: Classes for working with files and directories on the local file system.
- HttpClient and HttpServer: For making HTTP requests and serving HTTP content.
- Socket: Provides low-level network socket operations.
- stdin, stdout, and stderr: Standard input and output streams for command-line applications.

3. dart:html

The dart:html library is specific to web development in Dart. It allows you to interact with the Document Object Model (DOM) of a web page, manipulate HTML elements, and respond to user events. Some key components of this library include:

- HtmlDocument: Represents the HTML document itself.
- Element: The base class for all HTML elements, such as DivElement, AnchorElement, and more.
- Event: Provides a framework for working with events, including mouse clicks, keyboard input, and more.
- HttpRequest: For making HTTP requests from web applications.

4. dart:convert

The dart:convert library is essential for working with data serialization and deserialization. It provides encoders and decoders for various data formats, including JSON, UTF-8, and Base64. Key classes and functions include:

- json.decode() and json.encode(): Used to parse JSON strings into Dart objects and convert Dart objects into JSON strings.

- utf8.encode() and utf8.decode(): For handling UTF-8 encoding and decoding.

- base64.encode() and base64.decode(): Useful for working with Base64-encoded data.

These are just a few examples of the standard libraries available in Dart. As you delve deeper into Dart development, you'll discover many more libraries that can simplify your tasks and boost your productivity. Whether you're building web applications, server-side code, or mobile apps with Dart, understanding and utilizing these standard libraries is essential.

8.2 Third-Party Packages: Integration and Usage

While Dart's standard libraries provide a solid foundation for your projects, one of the strengths of the Dart ecosystem lies in its vibrant third-party package ecosystem. Dart's package manager, pub, allows you to easily integrate external packages into your projects, significantly expanding the functionality and efficiency of your applications.

In this section, we will explore how to work with third-party packages, integrate them into your Dart projects, and effectively utilize their features.

Installing Packages with pub

To begin using third-party packages, you'll need to use Dart's package manager, pub. Here's how you can install a package:

1. Open your project's pubspec.yaml file. This file is used to define project dependencies, including third-party packages.
2. Inside the dependencies section, add the package name and the desired version. For example:

```
dependencies:

http: ^3.0.0
```

In this example, we're specifying that we want to use the http package at version 3.0.0 or higher.

1. Save the pubspec.yaml file.
2. Run the pub get command in your project's root directory to fetch and install the specified package and its dependencies:

```
dart pub get
```

Importing and Using Packages

Once you've installed a package, you can import it into your Dart code using the import statement. For example, if you've installed the http package for making HTTP requests, you can import it like this:

```
import 'package:http/http.dart' as http;
```

The as keyword allows you to provide an alias for the imported library, which can be helpful to avoid naming conflicts with your existing code.

Example: Using the http Package

Let's look at a practical example of using the http package to make an HTTP GET request:

```
import 'package:http/http.dart' as http;

void main() async {

final response = await http.get(Uri.parse('https://jsonplaceholder.typicode.com/posts/1'));

if (response.statusCode == 200) {

print('Response data: ${response.body}');

} else {

print('Failed to load data. Status code: ${response.statusCode}');

}

}
```

In this code snippet:

- We import the http package with an alias http to avoid conflicts.

- We use the http.get function to make a GET request to a specified URL.

- We check the response's status code to determine if the request was successful and handle it accordingly.

Version Constraints

In your pubspec.yaml file, you can specify version constraints for packages. Dart supports various version constraint expressions, including:

- ^ (caret): Allows updates to the specified package version within the same major version.

- >= (greater than or equal): Specifies a minimum version.

- <= (less than or equal): Specifies a maximum version.

- > (greater than): Specifies a version higher than the specified one.

- < (less than): Specifies a version lower than the specified one.

Managing version constraints helps ensure that your project uses compatible package versions and reduces potential compatibility issues.

Package Documentation

Before using a third-party package, it's a good practice to consult the package's documentation. Package documentation typically includes examples, usage instructions, and information about the package's features and capabilities. The Dart package repository, pub.dev, hosts detailed documentation for most packages, making it a valuable resource for developers.

In conclusion, leveraging third-party packages in Dart can significantly accelerate your development process and expand the capabilities of your applications. By integrating packages using pub, importing them into your code, and understanding version constraints, you can harness the power of Dart's rich ecosystem to build robust and feature-rich applications.

8.3 Creating and Publishing Your Own Dart Package

In addition to using third-party packages, Dart allows you to create your own packages and publish them to the Dart package repository (pub.dev). This is incredibly useful when you want to share your code with others or reuse it across multiple projects. In this section, we will explore the process of creating and publishing your Dart package.

Creating a Dart Package

Creating a Dart package involves a series of steps:

1. **Package Structure**: A Dart package typically has a specific directory structure. Here's a basic structure for a Dart package:

```
my_package/
├── lib/
│   └── my_package.dart
```

├── pubspec.yaml

└── README.md

– The lib/ directory contains the Dart code for your package.

– The pubspec.yaml file defines package metadata and dependencies.

– The README.md file provides documentation and information about your package.

1. **Coding**: Write your Dart code inside the lib/ directory. You should have a primary Dart file (e.g., my_package.dart) that exports the functionality of your package.
2. **Pubspec Configuration**: In the pubspec.yaml file, specify your package's metadata, dependencies, and other information. Here's a minimal example:

name: my_package

version: 1.0.0

description: A sample Dart package

authors:

- Your Name <your@email.com>

1. **Documentation**: Create documentation for your package. This can be done using Dart's built-in documentation tool called dartdoc. Document your code using comments, and dartdoc will generate HTML documentation for your

package.
2. **Testing**: Write tests for your package using Dart's testing framework. Testing is crucial to ensure the correctness of your package's functionality.

Publishing Your Package

Once you've created your Dart package and ensured it's working correctly, you can publish it to pub.dev, Dart's package repository. Here are the steps to publish your package:

1. **Account Setup**: Ensure you have a Google account, as it's required to publish packages on pub.dev.
2. **Login to pub.dev**: Use the pub command-line tool to log in to your pub.dev account:

```
dart pub login
```

Follow the prompts to log in with your Google account.

1. **Package Version Bump**: Update the version of your package in the pubspec.yaml file. Dart uses semantic versioning, so follow the guidelines for version numbers.
2. **Publish the Package**: Use the following command to publish your package:

```
dart pub publish
```

This will upload your package to pub.dev.

1. **Documentation**: Ensure your package's documentation is up to date. The documentation generated by dartdoc will be available on pub.dev for others to view.
2. **Share Your Package**: Once published, you can share the

URL of your package on pub.dev with others. They can then add it as a dependency in their Dart projects.

Maintaining Your Package

Maintaining a published Dart package involves keeping it up to date, addressing issues, and collaborating with users. Here are some best practices for maintaining your package:

- Regularly update your package to support newer Dart versions and dependencies.
- Respond to issues and pull requests from users promptly.
- Consider adding tests and continuous integration to ensure the stability of your package.
- Keep your package's documentation clear and up to date.
- Engage with the Dart community to gather feedback and improve your package.

Creating and publishing your Dart packages can be a rewarding way to contribute to the Dart ecosystem and share your code with others. By following best practices and actively maintaining your packages, you can make a valuable contribution to the Dart developer community.

8.4 Package Management with Pub

In Dart, package management is essential for managing dependencies in your projects. Dart's package manager, pub, is a powerful tool for handling packages and dependencies. In this section, we will explore how to use pub for package management in Dart.

Understanding pubspec.yaml

Central to package management in Dart is the pubspec.yaml file. This file defines metadata about your Dart project, including its name, version, description, and dependencies. Here's an example of a pubspec.yaml file:

name: my_dart_project

version: 1.0.0

description: A sample Dart project

dependencies:

http: ^0.13.3

flutter: ^2.5.0

dev_dependencies:

test: ^2.15.6

- name: The name of your project.
- version: The version of your project.
- description: A short description of your project.
- dependencies: This section lists the packages that your project depends on. In the example above, it depends on the http package and the flutter framework. The ^ symbol indicates that the project is compatible with versions

greater than or equal to the specified version but less than the next major version.

• dev_dependencies: These are dependencies that are only required for development purposes. In the example above, the test package is used for writing tests.

Installing Dependencies

To install the dependencies listed in your pubspec.yaml file, run the following command in your project's directory:

dart pub get

This command reads the pubspec.yaml file, resolves dependencies, and fetches the packages from the Dart package repository (pub.dev). The packages are then stored in a directory called .dart_tool.

Upgrading Dependencies

You can upgrade your project's dependencies to their latest versions using the following command:

dart pub upgrade

This command updates the pubspec.yaml file with the latest compatible versions of your project's dependencies and fetches them from pub.dev.

Managing Dev Dependencies

Dev dependencies are typically used for development and testing purposes. To install dev dependencies, run:

dart pub get—dev

This command installs both regular dependencies and dev dependencies. To upgrade only dev dependencies, use:

dart pub upgrade—dev

Lock Files

When you run dart pub get or dart pub upgrade, pub generates a pubspec.lock file. This file records the exact versions of the packages that were resolved during the last dependency resolution. It ensures that you consistently use the same package versions across different development environments.

Publishing Your Own Packages

As discussed in Section 8.3, you can create and publish your own Dart packages to pub.dev. When other developers want to use your package, they can add it as a dependency in their project's pubspec.yaml file. This makes it easy to share code and collaborate within the Dart community.

In summary, pub is a powerful tool for managing dependencies in Dart projects. By defining dependencies in your pubspec.yaml file and using dart pub get or dart pub upgrade to fetch and update packages, you can streamline your development workflow and ensure your projects have access to the libraries and tools they need.

8.5 Keeping Your Code Updated and Secure

Keeping your Dart codebase updated and secure is crucial for maintaining a healthy and reliable software project. In this section, we'll discuss strategies and best practices for ensuring that your Dart projects are up-to-date and protected against security vulnerabilities.

Regularly Update Dependencies

One of the most critical aspects of maintaining code security and reliability is keeping your project's dependencies up to date. Dependencies can include third-party packages, libraries, and frameworks that your project relies on. Dart's package manager, pub, allows you to easily update your dependencies to the latest compatible versions.

To update your project's dependencies, run the following command in your project's directory:

dart pub upgrade

This command will check for newer versions of your project's dependencies and update the pubspec.yaml file accordingly. Regularly updating your dependencies ensures that you benefit from bug fixes, performance improvements, and security patches provided by the package maintainers.

Security Audits and Vulnerability Scanning

In addition to updating dependencies, consider using security auditing tools and services to identify and mitigate potential security vulnerabilities in your Dart code. Tools like OWASP Dependency-Check can help you scan your project for known vulnerabilities in your dependencies.

You can also explore services that offer automated vulnerability scanning for your code repositories, such as GitHub's Security Alerts. These services can alert you to security vulnerabilities in your project and provide guidance on how to address them.

Code Reviews and Static Analysis

Implementing code reviews as part of your development process is an effective way to catch security issues and maintain code quality. Peer code reviews allow experienced team members to assess code changes for security vulnerabilities, code smells, and best practices adherence.

Additionally, consider using static analysis tools like Dart's own dart analyze command or third-party tools like dartanalyzer to detect potential issues in your codebase. These tools can identify type errors, potential runtime exceptions, and other code problems early in the development process.

Stay Informed About Security Updates

To stay informed about security updates and best practices related to Dart and its ecosystem, subscribe to relevant mailing lists, forums, and news sources. The Dart community and package maintainers often release security advisories and updates to address vulnerabilities.

It's essential to monitor security announcements for both Dart itself and any third-party packages or libraries you use. When security updates are released, prioritize applying them to your projects to protect against potential threats.

Continuous Integration and Automated Testing

Implementing continuous integration (CI) and automated testing in your development workflow can help ensure that your codebase remains secure and reliable. CI tools can automatically build and test your code with each commit, providing rapid feedback on potential issues.

Consider including security-focused automated tests and vulnerability scanning as part of your CI pipeline. This helps you catch security vulnerabilities early in the development process and ensures that new code changes do not introduce security regressions.

Conclusion

Maintaining code security and reliability in your Dart projects requires a proactive approach. Regularly updating dependencies, conducting security audits, performing code reviews, staying informed about security updates, and implementing CI and automated testing are all essential practices to keep your codebase secure and up-to-date.

By following these best practices, you can mitigate security risks, deliver high-quality software, and contribute to a safer and more robust Dart development ecosystem.

Chapter 9: Interfacing with Other Languages

9.1 Dart and JavaScript: Bridging the Gap

Dart is a versatile language that can interact with various other programming languages. One of the most common scenarios is interfacing with JavaScript. This interoperation is crucial when you want to utilize existing JavaScript libraries, frameworks, or APIs within your Dart application or vice versa. In this section, we will explore how Dart and JavaScript can seamlessly work together.

The JavaScript Interop Library

Dart provides a dedicated package called js for interacting with JavaScript. This package enables you to seamlessly call JavaScript functions, access JavaScript objects, and exchange data between Dart and JavaScript.

To use the js package in your Dart project, add it as a dependency in your pubspec.yaml file:

dependencies:

js: ^0.6.1

After adding the dependency, run dart pub get to fetch the package.

Importing JavaScript Code

To use JavaScript code in your Dart application, you need to import it using the dart:js library. Here's how you can do it:

import 'dart:js' as js;

This import allows you to access JavaScript objects and functions via the js object.

Calling JavaScript Functions

You can call JavaScript functions from Dart using the callMethod method provided by the js object. Here's an example of calling a JavaScript function named sayHello:

```
js.context.callMethod('sayHello', ['Dart']);
```

In this example, we use js.context to access the global JavaScript context, and we call the sayHello function with the argument 'Dart'.

Accessing JavaScript Objects

You can also access JavaScript objects and their properties from Dart using the [] operator. For instance, if you have a JavaScript object person with a property name, you can access it like this:

```
var person = js.context['person'];

var name = person['name'];
```

JavaScript Promises and Futures

When working with asynchronous JavaScript code that returns promises, you can await them in Dart using the js.promiseToFuture function. This allows you to work with JavaScript promises as if they were Dart futures. Here's an example:

```
var jsPromise = js.context.callMethod('fetchData');

var dartFuture = js.promiseToFuture(jsPromise);

dartFuture.then((result) {
```

```
print('Data fetched: $result');
}).catchError((error) {
print('Error fetching data: $error');
});
```

Interoperability Caveats

While Dart's JavaScript interop capabilities are powerful, there are some caveats to keep in mind:

1. **Type Safety**: JavaScript is dynamically typed, while Dart is statically typed. Be cautious when working with untyped JavaScript values to avoid runtime errors.
2. **Null Safety**: Dart introduced null safety, which may lead to issues when interacting with JavaScript, where null is often used to represent missing values. Pay attention to handling null values when interfacing with JavaScript.
3. **Garbage Collection**: Dart has its garbage collector, while JavaScript relies on the browser's garbage collector. Be mindful of object lifecycles when passing objects between Dart and JavaScript.
4. **Debugging**: Debugging Dart and JavaScript interop can be challenging. Use browser developer tools and Dart DevTools to aid in debugging.

Conclusion

Interfacing with JavaScript is essential for leveraging existing web libraries and APIs in your Dart applications. Dart's js package and the dart:js library provide powerful tools for bridging the gap between Dart and JavaScript. Understanding the interoperation techniques and being mindful of potential pitfalls will enable you to create seamless and efficient cross-language applications.

9.2 Calling C and C++ Code from Dart

Dart's versatility extends beyond web development and JavaScript interoperability. It also allows you to interface with code written in languages like C and C++. This capability is particularly useful when you need to utilize existing native libraries, optimize performance-critical tasks, or work with low-level hardware. In this section, we will explore how to call C and C++ code from Dart using the Dart FFI (Foreign Function Interface) library.

Dart FFI (Foreign Function Interface)

Dart FFI is a powerful tool that enables you to interact with native code written in C or C++ from Dart. It provides a bridge between the Dart runtime and native libraries, allowing you to call functions, access data structures, and manage memory.

To use Dart FFI, you need to add the ffi package as a dependency in your Dart project's pubspec.yaml file:

dependencies:

ffi: ^1.0.0

After adding the dependency, run dart pub get to fetch the package.

Creating a Dart FFI Library

To call C/C++ code from Dart, you must create a Dart FFI library. This library defines the Dart functions that correspond to the C/ C++ functions you want to use. It also specifies the dynamic library (shared object or DLL) that contains the native code.

Here's an example of a Dart FFI library that calls a C function:

```
import 'dart:ffi'; // Import the Dart FFI library

import 'dart:io' show Platform; // Import the Platform library for OS-specific dynamic library loading

final DynamicLibrary nativeLibrary = Platform.isLinux

? DynamicLibrary.open('libnative.so') // Linux

: (Platform.isMacOS

? DynamicLibrary.open('libnative.dylib') // macOS

: DynamicLibrary.open('native.dll')); // Windows

// Define the Dart FFI function signature

typedef SumC = Int32 Function(Int32, Int32);

typedef SumDart = int Function(int, int);

void main() {

final sum = nativeLibrary

.lookupFunction<SumC, SumDart>('sum'); // Look up the C function 'sum'

final result = sum(3, 5); // Call the 'sum' function

print('Sum of 3 and 5: $result');

}
```

In this example, we define the Dart FFI library, specify the dynamic library file to load based on the platform, and define the function signature for a C function named sum. We then use lookupFunction to map the C function to a Dart function and call it.

Handling Data Types

Dart FFI provides a set of types for mapping between Dart and C/C++ data types, including integers, floating-point numbers, strings, and custom structs. You can use these types to pass data between Dart and native code seamlessly.

Memory Management

Managing memory is crucial when working with Dart FFI, especially when allocating or freeing memory in C/C++ functions. Dart FFI provides tools like calloc, malloc, and free for memory allocation and deallocation.

Error Handling

Dart FFI functions can throw exceptions if they encounter issues during execution. It's essential to handle these exceptions properly to prevent crashes and memory leaks.

Conclusion

Calling C and C++ code from Dart opens up opportunities for leveraging native libraries, optimizing performance-critical tasks, and interfacing with low-level hardware. Dart FFI provides a robust mechanism for bridging the gap between Dart and native code, enabling developers to create cross-language applications that combine the power of Dart with the capabilities of C and C++. Understanding data types, memory management, and error handling is crucial when working with Dart FFI to ensure safe and efficient interoperation.

9.3 Dart FFI (Foreign Function Interface)

Dart FFI (Foreign Function Interface) is a powerful feature that allows Dart code to interact with native code written in languages like C and C++. This capability enables you to leverage existing libraries and access low-level system functionality, making Dart a versatile choice for various application domains.

Using Dart FFI

To use Dart FFI, you need to import the dart:ffi library, which provides the necessary tools for working with native code. You'll also need to add the ffi package to your Dart project's pubspec.yaml file and run dart pub get to fetch the package.

Here's a basic example of using Dart FFI to call a C function that calculates the factorial of a number:

```
import 'dart:ffi'; // Import the Dart FFI library

final DynamicLibrary nativeLibrary =
DynamicLibrary.open('my_native_library.so');

typedef FactorialC = Int64 Function(Int32);

typedef FactorialDart = int Function(int);

void main() {

final factorial = nativeLibrary

.lookupFunction<FactorialC, FactorialDart>('calculate_factorial');

final result = factorial(5); // Calculate the factorial of 5

print('Factorial of 5 is $result');
```

```
}
```

In this example, we define the Dart FFI library, specify the dynamic library file (e.g., a shared object or DLL) that contains the native code, and declare the function signature for the C function calculate_factorial. We then use lookupFunction to map the C function to a Dart function and call it.

Data Types and Conversions

Dart FFI provides data types to represent C/C++ types, including integers, floating-point numbers, pointers, and structures. You can use these types to define function signatures and exchange data between Dart and native code.

For instance, Int32 corresponds to a 32-bit integer, and Double represents a double-precision floating-point number. Dart FFI also provides Pointer for working with memory pointers and Struct for defining custom data structures.

Memory Management

When interacting with native code, you may need to allocate and deallocate memory. Dart FFI provides functions like calloc and malloc for memory allocation and free for memory deallocation.

It's crucial to manage memory properly to prevent memory leaks and ensure your application's stability.

Error Handling

Dart FFI functions can throw exceptions if they encounter issues during execution, such as null pointer access or invalid memory operations. Proper error handling is essential to handle these exceptions and maintain the reliability of your code.

Conclusion

Dart FFI is a valuable feature that enhances Dart's capabilities by enabling interactions with native code. Whether you need to use existing C/C++ libraries, optimize performance-critical tasks, or access low-level system functionality, Dart FFI provides the tools you need. Understanding data types, memory management, and error handling is essential when working with Dart FFI to ensure safe and efficient communication between Dart and native code.

9.4 Mobile Platform Integration: Android and iOS

Dart provides a robust ecosystem for mobile app development, particularly when combined with Google's UI toolkit, Flutter. Flutter allows you to build natively compiled applications for mobile from a single codebase. In this section, we'll explore how you can integrate Dart, Flutter, and platform-specific code to target both Android and iOS platforms.

Flutter for Cross-Platform Development

One of Dart's strengths is its integration with Flutter. Flutter is an open-source framework developed by Google that simplifies cross-platform app development. It provides a rich set of widgets and tools for creating beautiful and performant mobile apps.

To get started with Flutter, you need to install the Flutter SDK and set up your development environment. Once you have Flutter installed, you can create a new Flutter project using the flutter create command. This command generates the project structure, including platform-specific directories for Android and iOS.

Platform Channels

Flutter allows you to integrate platform-specific code using platform channels. Platform channels enable communication between your Dart code and native code written in Java (for Android) or Swift/Objective-C (for iOS).

You can use platform channels to perform platform-specific tasks that cannot be accomplished with pure Dart code. This includes accessing device sensors, interacting with platform-specific APIs, and integrating third-party native libraries.

Here's an example of how you can use platform channels to display a native dialog on Android and iOS:

```
import 'package:flutter/material.dart';

import 'package:flutter/services.dart';

void main() {

runApp(MyApp());

}

class MyApp extends StatelessWidget {

@override

Widget build(BuildContext context) {

return MaterialApp(

home: Scaffold(

appBar: AppBar(

title: Text('Platform Channels Example'),
```

```
),
body: Center(
child: ElevatedButton(
onPressed: () {
_showNativeDialog();
},
child: Text('Show Native Dialog'),
),
),
),
);
}
// Method to show a native dialog using platform channels
Future<void> _showNativeDialog() async {
const platform = MethodChannel('my_flutter_app/dialog');
try {
await platform.invokeMethod('showDialog', 'Hello from Flutter!');
} on PlatformException catch (e) {
print('Error: ${e.message}');
}
```

```
}
}
```

In this example, we use the MethodChannel class to create a platform channel named 'my_flutter_app/dialog'. When the button is pressed, the _showNativeDialog method invokes the 'showDialog' method on the platform channel, passing a message. Native code on Android and iOS can listen to this method call and display a platform-specific dialog.

Platform-Specific Implementations

To make platform-specific implementations, you'll need to write native code for Android and iOS. In Android, you can use Java or Kotlin, while in iOS, you can use Swift or Objective-C. These implementations should listen to method calls on the platform channel and perform the required platform-specific actions.

Conclusion

Dart and Flutter provide a powerful platform for mobile app development, allowing you to target both Android and iOS from a single codebase. By using platform channels, you can seamlessly integrate platform-specific functionality into your Flutter app, ensuring a consistent user experience across different devices and operating systems.

9.5 Exploring Other Language Interoperability

Dart's interoperability capabilities extend beyond its ability to work with JavaScript and native platform code. You can also explore interoperability with other languages, which can be particularly valuable when you have existing codebases or libraries in those languages that you want to leverage in your Dart projects. In this section, we'll briefly explore some of the possibilities for language interoperability in Dart.

Using Dart FFI

Dart FFI (Foreign Function Interface) allows you to call functions from dynamic libraries written in C and other languages. This opens up opportunities for integrating existing C libraries or libraries from other languages into your Dart applications. Dart FFI provides a bridge between Dart and native code, making it possible to use shared libraries without rewriting them in Dart.

To use Dart FFI, you need to import the dart:ffi library and declare the functions you want to call from the native library. Here's a simplified example of how you can use Dart FFI to call a function from a C library:

```
import 'dart:ffi'; // Import the dart:ffi library

import 'package:ffi/ffi.dart';

// Define the Dynamic Library interface

final myLibrary = DynamicLibrary.open('my_library.so'); // Load the C library

// Define the C function signature

typedef MyFunction = Int32 Function(Int32 a, Int32 b);

typedef MyFunctionDart = int Function(int a, int b);

void main() {

// Convert the Dart function to a C function
```

```
final myFunction = myLibrary

.lookupFunction<MyFunction, MyFunctionDart>('myFunction');

// Call the C function

final result = myFunction(5, 7);

print('Result: $result');

}
```

In this example, we load a C dynamic library (my_library.so) using DynamicLibrary.open. We then define the C function's signature using typedef, and finally, we use lookupFunction to convert the C function into a Dart function that we can call.

Interoperability with Other Languages

While Dart FFI is primarily designed for C interop, you can explore using Dart with other languages as well. For example:

- **Rust**: Rust has a Foreign Function Interface (FFI) that allows you to create C-compatible APIs. You can use Dart FFI to call Rust functions if you create a C-compatible Rust library.

- **Python**: You can use the PyDart package to call Python code from Dart. This can be useful for integrating machine learning models or leveraging Python libraries.

- **Go**: Go provides a C-compatible FFI, allowing you to call Go functions from Dart using Dart FFI. This can be useful for accessing Go libraries and services.

- **Java/Kotlin**: If you're working on Android applications using Flutter, you can use platform channels to invoke Java or Kotlin code from Dart.

The feasibility of using other languages with Dart depends on the language's FFI capabilities and whether there are existing libraries or tools that facilitate interoperability.

Conclusion

Dart's flexibility extends to its ability to interoperate with other languages, making it a versatile choice for a wide range of projects. Whether you need to leverage existing code or libraries from other languages or explore unique integration opportunities, Dart's interoperability features provide you with the tools to do so. Keep in mind that successful language interoperability may require understanding the specifics of both Dart and the target language's FFI capabilities.

Chapter 10: Advanced UI with Flutter

10.1 Advanced Widgets and Layouts in Flutter

In Flutter, building beautiful and interactive user interfaces (UI) is a breeze, thanks to its rich set of widgets and powerful layout system. While you may have already worked with basic widgets like Text, Image, and Button, this section delves into the world of advanced widgets and complex layouts, allowing you to create stunning and responsive UIs for your Flutter applications.

Introduction to Advanced Widgets

Flutter provides a wide range of advanced widgets that go beyond the basics and cater to more specific UI requirements. Some of these widgets include:

- **ListView**: When you need to create scrollable lists of items, the ListView widget comes in handy. It allows you to display a large number of items efficiently by rendering only the visible ones.

- **GridView**: Similar to ListView, GridView is used to display a collection of items, but it arranges them in a grid layout. You can customize the number of columns and the alignment of items.

- **TabBar and TabView**: If your app requires a tabbed interface, you can use TabBar and TabView widgets to create a tabbed layout easily. Each tab can display different content.

- **ExpansionPanel**: When you want to show collapsible panels, Flutter offers the ExpansionPanel widget. It allows users to expand and collapse content sections as needed.

- **Stepper**: The Stepper widget is perfect for guiding users through a multi-step process. You can create step-by-step forms or wizards with ease.

Advanced Layouts

Building complex layouts is a crucial part of UI design, and Flutter provides a flexible and powerful layout system to achieve this. Some advanced layout concepts include:

- **Row and Column**: These are fundamental widgets for arranging children in horizontal (Row) and vertical (Column) sequences. You can use them in combination to create intricate layouts.

- **Stack**: The Stack widget lets you overlay widgets on top of each other. This is useful for creating overlapping UI elements, such as floating action buttons.

- **Expanded and Flexible**: These widgets are essential for controlling how space is distributed among children within Row and Column layouts. They help in creating responsive designs.

- **CustomPaint**: For custom drawings and graphics, you can use the CustomPaint widget. It allows you to create custom shapes, charts, and diagrams by painting on a canvas.

Responsive Design

Designing UIs that adapt to different screen sizes and orientations is critical in today's mobile and web applications. Flutter offers several techniques for achieving responsive design:

- **MediaQuery**: You can use the MediaQuery class to access information about the device's screen size, orientation, and more. This information is useful for making layout decisions.

- **LayoutBuilder**: The LayoutBuilder widget allows you to create layouts that respond to their parent's constraints. It provides you with constraints information to adapt your layout accordingly.

- **FractionallySizedBox**: This widget lets you specify dimensions as fractions of the parent widget's size. It's handy for creating UI components that should occupy a portion of the available space.

Conclusion

With the knowledge of advanced widgets and layout techniques, you have the tools to design and implement sophisticated user interfaces in your Flutter applications. Whether you need to create complex layouts, handle responsiveness, or build custom UI components, Flutter's extensive widget library and flexible layout system have you covered. In the upcoming sections of this chapter, we'll dive deeper into specific aspects of advanced UI development in Flutter, including custom animations, multimedia integration, and support for desktop and web applications.

10.2 Custom Animation and Motion Design

Animation and motion design are essential components of modern user interfaces. They bring life to your Flutter applications, making them more engaging and visually appealing. In this section, we'll explore how to create custom animations and incorporate motion design into your Flutter UI.

Animation Basics

In Flutter, animations are achieved by changing the properties of widgets over time. To get started with animations, you need to understand some core concepts:

- **Animation Controller**: An animation controller manages the animation's lifecycle, including starting, stopping, and controlling the animation's progress. It also defines the duration and curve of the animation.

- **Animation**: An animation represents a value that changes over time. Flutter provides various types of animations, including Animation<double>, Animation<Color>, and more. You can interpolate these animations to achieve different effects.

- **Tween:** A tween defines the range of values that an animation should animate between. For example, a Tween<double> may go from 0.0 to 1.0, and a Tween<Color> may transition between two colors.

Using Animated Widgets

Flutter offers a set of pre-built animated widgets that simplify common animation tasks. These widgets automatically manage animations for you. Some notable ones include:

- **AnimatedContainer**: This widget smoothly transitions between different sizes, colors, and shapes. It's useful for animating changes in widget properties.

- **AnimatedOpacity**: When you need to fade a widget in or out, AnimatedOpacity is the go-to choice. It gradually changes the widget's opacity.

- **Hero**: The Hero widget enables hero animations, which are animations that transition widgets from one screen to another. It's often used for transitioning images and text between screens.

Creating Custom Animations

While the built-in animated widgets are convenient for many cases, you may need to create custom animations for unique UI effects. Flutter provides the CustomPainter class, which allows you to paint custom graphics and animations onto a canvas.

Here's a simplified example of creating a custom animation using the CustomPainter class:

```
class MyCustomPainter extends CustomPainter {

final Animation<double> animation;

MyCustomPainter({required this.animation}) : super(repaint: animation);
```

```
@override
void paint(Canvas canvas, Size size) {
final radius = 30.0 + 20.0 * animation.value;
final paint = Paint()..color = Colors.blue;
final center = Offset(size.width / 2, size.height / 2);
canvas.drawCircle(center, radius, paint);
}
@override
bool shouldRepaint(CustomPainter oldDelegate) => false;
}
```

In this example, we define a custom painter that draws a circle whose radius changes based on the provided animation. The super(repaint: animation) line ensures that the animation controller triggers repaints when the animation updates.

Motion Design and Physics

Creating realistic motion in your Flutter animations often involves applying physics-based animations. The flutter_physics package provides physics-based animations that simulate real-world behavior like springs and flings. These can be applied to achieve natural-feeling animations in your UI.

Conclusion

Custom animations and motion design are powerful tools for enhancing your Flutter applications. Whether you need to create unique UI effects, transition between screens, or apply physics-based animations, Flutter offers the flexibility and tools to bring your designs to life. In the next section, we'll explore integrating multimedia elements into your Flutter apps, further enriching the user experience.

10.3 Integrating Multimedia Elements

Multimedia elements such as images, audio, and video play a vital role in creating rich and engaging user interfaces in Flutter. In this section, we'll explore how to integrate multimedia elements into your Flutter applications, making them more dynamic and interactive.

Displaying Images

Images are a fundamental part of most user interfaces. Flutter provides several widgets for displaying images, with the most common one being the Image widget. To display a local image, you can use the AssetImage or FileImage class to load images from your project's assets or the device's file system, respectively.

Here's an example of displaying an image using the Image widget:

```
Image.asset('assets/images/logo.png', width: 100, height: 100)
```

This code loads an image named 'logo.png' from the 'assets/images' directory and sets its dimensions.

Adding Icons

Icons are essential for conveying information and actions in your app. Flutter includes a wide range of icons through the Icons class, and you can use the Icon widget to display them.

Icon(Icons.star, color: Colors.yellow, size: 32)

This code displays a yellow star icon with a size of 32 pixels.

Audio Playback

For audio playback, Flutter offers the audioplayers package, which provides a straightforward way to play audio files. You can use it to play local audio files or stream audio from the internet.

Here's a simple example of using the audioplayers package to play an audio file:

import 'package:audioplayers/audio_cache.dart';

final player = AudioCache();

player.play('audio/song.mp3');

This code imports the audioplayers package, creates an AudioCache instance, and plays the 'song.mp3' file from the 'audio' directory.

Video Playback

To integrate video playback into your Flutter app, you can use the video_player package. It provides a widget called VideoPlayerController that allows you to display and control videos.

Here's a basic example of how to play a video using the video_player package:

import 'package:video_player/video_player.dart';

final videoController = VideoPlayerController.asset('assets/videos/sample.mp4');

VideoPlayer(videoController)

This code imports the video_player package, creates a VideoPlayerController for a video asset, and displays it using the VideoPlayer widget.

Camera and Augmented Reality (AR)

For apps that require camera access and AR capabilities, Flutter provides packages like camera and arcore_flutter_plugin. These packages enable you to capture photos and videos, as well as create AR experiences within your app.

Using these packages, you can access device cameras, display live camera feeds, and even overlay AR objects onto the camera view.

Conclusion

Integrating multimedia elements into your Flutter applications opens up a world of possibilities for creating visually appealing and interactive user interfaces. Whether you need to display images, play audio and video, or harness the power of AR, Flutter provides the tools and packages to bring multimedia experiences to life. In the next section, we'll explore the principles of responsive and adaptive design, ensuring that your Flutter apps look great on various devices and screen sizes.

10.4 Responsive and Adaptive Design Principles

Creating Flutter applications that look and function well across a variety of devices and screen sizes is crucial for providing a consistent user experience. In this section, we'll delve into responsive and adaptive design principles in Flutter, helping you ensure your app adapts gracefully to different form factors.

Understanding Responsiveness

Responsiveness is the ability of your Flutter app to adjust its layout and content to different screen sizes and orientations. Achieving responsiveness involves designing your UI components and layouts to be flexible and adaptable.

Using Layout Builders

The LayoutBuilder widget is a powerful tool for creating responsive layouts. It allows you to build your UI based on the constraints provided by its parent. By examining the constraints, you can make decisions about how your widgets should be sized and positioned.

Here's an example of using LayoutBuilder to create a responsive layout:

```
LayoutBuilder(
builder: (BuildContext context, BoxConstraints constraints) {
if (constraints.maxWidth > 600) {
return DesktopLayout();
} else {
return MobileLayout();
}
},
)
```

In this code, we check the maximum width of the available space and choose between a desktop or mobile layout accordingly.

Adaptive Layouts

While responsiveness focuses on adjusting to various screen sizes, **adaptive design** takes into account different device types and their unique capabilities. Flutter makes it easy to create adaptive layouts that cater to specific platforms, such as mobile, tablet, and desktop.

Platform-Specific Widgets

Flutter provides platform-specific widgets that adapt to the conventions and design guidelines of each platform. For instance, you can use the Cupertino widgets for iOS-style design and Material widgets for Android-style design. Flutter automatically adapts these widgets based on the target platform.

```
import 'package:flutter/cupertino.dart' as cupertino;

import 'package:flutter/material.dart' as material;

// Platform-specific widget usage

if (isIOS) {

return cupertino.CupertinoButton(

child: Text('iOS Button'),

onPressed: () {},

);

} else {

return material.TextButton(

child: Text('Android Button'),
```

```
onPressed: () {},
);
}
```

Here, we conditionally choose between CupertinoButton and TextButton based on the platform.

Handling Orientation Changes

Adaptive design also involves handling changes in device orientation. You can listen to orientation changes using the OrientationBuilder widget or the MediaQuery class. When the orientation changes, you can update your UI accordingly.

Conclusion

Creating responsive and adaptive Flutter apps ensures that users have a consistent and enjoyable experience, no matter which device they use. By utilizing LayoutBuilder, platform-specific widgets, and handling orientation changes, you can tailor your app to various screen sizes and platforms. In the next section, we'll explore Flutter's capabilities for desktop and web applications, extending the reach of your projects beyond mobile devices.

10.5 Flutter for Desktop and Web Applications

Flutter's versatility extends beyond mobile app development, allowing you to build applications for desktop and the web as well. In this section, we'll explore how you can leverage Flutter to create high-quality desktop and web applications.

Desktop Support with Flutter

Flutter enables you to build desktop applications for Windows, macOS, and Linux using the same codebase as your mobile app. This cross-platform compatibility is made possible by the Flutter desktop project, which provides platform-specific plugins and libraries for desktop development.

Setting Up Flutter for Desktop

To get started with desktop development, you need to configure your Flutter project for desktop platforms. Follow these steps to set up Flutter for desktop:

1. Ensure you have Flutter installed.
2. Run the following command to enable desktop support:

flutter config—enable-windows-desktop

flutter config—enable-macos-desktop

flutter config—enable-linux-desktop

1. Create or navigate to a Flutter project and run your app on the desktop platform of your choice:

flutter run -d windows

flutter run -d macos

flutter run -d linux

Designing for Desktop

When designing for desktop, consider the larger screen size and different interaction patterns compared to mobile devices. You can use platform-specific widgets and layouts to provide a native-like experience on each desktop platform.

```
import 'package:flutter/material.dart';

class DesktopApp extends StatelessWidget {

@override

Widget build(BuildContext context) {

return Scaffold(

body: Center(

child: Text(

'Desktop Application',

style: TextStyle(fontSize: 24),

),

),

);

}

}
```

Web Support with Flutter

Flutter also allows you to build web applications, expanding your reach to users on web browsers. Flutter's web support is still in development, but it offers exciting opportunities for building web applications with the same codebase.

Setting Up Flutter for Web

To enable web support in your Flutter project, follow these steps:

1. Ensure you have Flutter installed.
2. Run the following command to enable web support:

```
flutter config—enable-web
```

1. Create or navigate to a Flutter project and run your app on the web:

```
flutter run -d web
```

Building for the Web

While Flutter for web shares many widgets and libraries with mobile development, it's essential to consider the web's unique characteristics. Optimize your web app for responsiveness, browser compatibility, and performance. Flutter's web support offers tools to help you achieve these goals.

```
import 'package:flutter/material.dart';

void main() {

runApp(MyApp());
```

```
}
class MyApp extends StatelessWidget {
@override
Widget build(BuildContext context) {
return MaterialApp(
title: 'Flutter Web App',
theme: ThemeData(
primarySwatch: Colors.blue,
),
home: MyHomePage(),
);
}
}
```

Conclusion

Flutter's ability to target desktop and web platforms alongside mobile makes it a powerful framework for cross-platform development. Whether you're building a desktop application for multiple operating systems or expanding your app to the web, Flutter provides a consistent and efficient development experience. In the following chapters, we'll explore more advanced topics and use cases for Flutter, empowering you to build even more sophisticated and feature-rich applications.

Chapter 11: State Management in Dart

Section 11.1: Understanding State Management

State management is a critical aspect of building robust and maintainable applications, and it plays a central role in Dart app development. In this section, we'll delve into the fundamentals of state management, exploring why it's essential and how it influences the structure and behavior of Dart applications.

The Significance of State

At its core, state represents the data or information that an application needs to function. It includes variables, objects, or values that define the current condition or context of the app. Understanding state is crucial because it determines how your application responds to user interactions and external events.

State in Dart Applications

In Dart, state is ubiquitous. It can be as simple as the visibility of a button or as complex as the contents of a database. Dart applications must manage different types of state, including:

1. **Local State:** This state is specific to a particular widget or component in your app. For example, the text entered into a text field or the selected item in a dropdown menu are local states.
2. **Global State:** Global state is shared across multiple parts of your app, often requiring synchronization. Examples include user authentication status, theme settings, or data fetched from an API.

Challenges of State Management

State management can be challenging due to the following factors:

- **Complexity:** As an app grows, so does the complexity of managing its state. You must ensure that state changes are reflected accurately throughout the app.

- **Concurrency:** In a multi-threaded environment, handling state changes concurrently can lead to race conditions and bugs.

- **Maintainability:** Poorly managed state can make your codebase hard to maintain, debug, and extend.

State Management Techniques

There are several techniques for managing state in Dart applications, each with its strengths and weaknesses:

1. **Local State Management:** This involves managing state within individual widgets or components. It's suitable for simple cases but can become unwieldy for complex apps.
2. **Inherited Widget:** Dart provides the InheritedWidget class, which allows you to propagate state down the widget tree. It's useful for sharing state among multiple widgets.
3. **Provider Package:** The Provider package is a popular choice for state management in Flutter applications. It offers a flexible and efficient way to manage both local and global state.
4. **BLoC (Business Logic Component) Pattern:** BLoC is a design pattern that separates the business logic from the user interface. It's well-suited for managing complex state and asynchronous operations.

5. **Redux:** Redux is a state management library inspired by JavaScript's Redux. It enforces a unidirectional data flow and is favored by developers experienced with Redux.
6. **GetX:** GetX is a lightweight yet powerful state management solution for Flutter. It provides reactive state management, dependency injection, and routing capabilities.

Selecting the Right State Management Approach

The choice of state management technique depends on the complexity of your app and your team's familiarity with different patterns. Simple apps may benefit from local state management, while larger and more complex projects might require the structure and scalability provided by solutions like Provider, BLoC, or Redux.

In the following sections, we'll dive deeper into specific state management techniques, examining their implementation and best practices.

By the end of this chapter, you'll have a solid understanding of how to manage state effectively in your Dart applications, enabling you to create responsive and maintainable software.

Section 11.2: Global State vs Local State

In the realm of state management in Dart applications, one of the fundamental distinctions to be made is between global state and local state. Both types of state serve essential roles within your app, and understanding when to use each is key to building maintainable and efficient software.

Global State

Global state, as the name suggests, is state that is accessible and modifiable from various parts of your application. It is shared across multiple widgets, screens, or components. Global state is typically used for data that needs to be consistent and synchronized across different parts of your app, such as user authentication status, user preferences, or fetched data from a remote server.

Advantages of Global State:

1. **Accessibility:** Since global state is accessible from anywhere in your app, it simplifies data sharing among widgets that are not directly related in the widget tree.
2. **Consistency:** Global state ensures that data remains consistent and up-to-date throughout your app, reducing the risk of inconsistencies or synchronization issues.
3. **Centralization:** It centralizes the management of critical data, making it easier to implement features like dark mode, user authentication, or language preferences.

Challenges of Global State:

1. **Complexity:** Managing global state can become complex as your app grows. It's crucial to have a clear structure and organization to prevent confusion.
2. **Performance:** Excessive reliance on global state can lead to performance bottlenecks, as every widget that depends on the state must rebuild when it changes.
3. **Testing:** Testing global state interactions and changes can be challenging, as you need to ensure that state changes propagate correctly.

Local State

Local state, on the other hand, is confined to a specific widget or component. It is private to that widget and is not directly accessible from other parts of the app. Local state is typically used for widget-specific data or transient information that doesn't need to be shared globally. Examples include the state of a checkbox, the progress of an animation, or the value of a text input.

Advantages of Local State:

1. **Isolation:** Local state is isolated to a specific widget, making it self-contained and easy to reason about. Changes in local state have minimal impact on other parts of the app.
2. **Predictability:** Since local state is confined, it is predictable and less likely to cause unexpected side effects or bugs.
3. **Performance:** Widgets with local state can rebuild independently when their state changes, improving performance by avoiding unnecessary widget rebuilds.

Challenges of Local State:

1. **Sharing Data:** In some cases, you may need to share data between widgets that have local state. Managing the communication and synchronization of local state across multiple widgets can be challenging.
2. **Consistency:** Local state can lead to inconsistencies if not properly managed. For example, two widgets may have their local state that represents the same piece of information, leading to synchronization issues.

Choosing Between Global and Local State

The decision to use global or local state depends on the specific requirements of your app and the data in question. Consider the following guidelines:

- Use global state for data that needs to be shared and synchronized across different parts of your app, such as user authentication, language preferences, or fetched data.

- Use local state for widget-specific data that doesn't need to be accessed or modified by other widgets. This keeps your widgets isolated and helps maintain a clear separation of concerns.

- In some cases, a combination of both global and local state may be the best approach. For example, you can use global state to manage user authentication status while using local state for widget-specific UI interactions.

In the next sections, we'll explore state management techniques in Dart that facilitate the effective management of both global and local state.

Section 11.3: Popular State Management Techniques

In Dart and Flutter, several state management techniques have emerged over the years to help developers manage the state of their applications effectively. Each technique has its strengths and is suited to different scenarios. Here, we'll explore some popular state management approaches commonly used by Flutter developers.

1. setState()

The setState() method is the simplest form of state management in Flutter. It is used for managing the state within a single widget. When you call setState(), Flutter rebuilds the widget and its descendants, updating the UI to reflect the new state.

```
int _counter = 0;

void _incrementCounter() {

setState(() {

_counter++;

});

}
```

Pros:

- Simplicity: setState() is straightforward and easy to use for managing local state within a widget.

Cons:

- Limited Scope: It's not suitable for managing state that needs to be shared across multiple widgets or for large-scale applications as it doesn't provide a global state management solution.

2. InheritedWidget

InheritedWidget is a widget that allows data to be passed down the widget tree efficiently. It's the foundation for several state management libraries in Flutter, including Provider and Riverpod.

By wrapping widgets with InheritedWidget, you can propagate data to descendant widgets without explicitly passing it as arguments.

```
class MyInheritedWidget extends InheritedWidget {

const MyInheritedWidget({

Key? key,

required Widget child,

required this.data,

}) : super(key: key, child: child);

final int data;

static MyInheritedWidget of(BuildContext context) {

return
context.dependOnInheritedWidgetOfExactType<MyInheritedWidget>()!

}

@override

bool updateShouldNotify(covariant InheritedWidget oldWidget) {

return true;

}

}
```

Pros:

- Efficient Data Propagation: InheritedWidget efficiently passes data down the widget tree without excessive widget reconstruction.

- Simplicity: It's relatively simple and doesn't require additional packages for basic use cases.

Cons:

- Limited to Descendants: Data can only be accessed by descendant widgets in the widget tree, making it less suitable for global state management.

3. Provider

Provider is a state management solution that builds on top of InheritedWidget. It provides a convenient way to manage and access state within your Flutter app. With Provider, you can easily share state across different parts of your app, from widgets to services.

```
final counterProvider = Provider<int>((ref) => 0);

class MyWidget extends StatelessWidget {

@override

Widget build(BuildContext context) {

final counter = context.read(counterProvider);

// ...

}

}
```

Pros:

- Easy to Use: Provider simplifies state management and reduces boilerplate code.

- Scalable: It's suitable for both local and global state management, making it versatile for various app sizes.

Cons:

- Learning Curve: Understanding the nuances of Provider and its associated packages may take time for newcomers.

4. Bloc Pattern (with Flutter Bloc)

The Bloc pattern is a state management approach that separates business logic from the presentation layer. In Flutter, the flutter_bloc package provides tools to implement the Bloc pattern effectively. It's especially well-suited for complex applications where state changes are tied to specific events.

```
class CounterCubit extends Cubit<int> {

CounterCubit() : super(0);

void increment() => emit(state + 1);

}
```

Pros:

- Separation of Concerns: The Bloc pattern enforces a clear separation of business logic from UI, making code more maintainable and testable.

- Reactive: It embraces a reactive programming style, which is beneficial for handling complex state changes.

Cons:

• Complexity: Implementing the Bloc pattern may seem more complex, especially for simple applications.

5. GetX

GetX is a lightweight Flutter package that offers both state management and dependency injection capabilities. It is known for its simplicity and performance. GetX allows you to manage state, routes, and more, all in a single package.

```
final count = 0.obs;

void increment() => count.value++;
```

Pros:

• Minimal Boilerplate: GetX requires minimal setup and reduces boilerplate code.

• Performance: It is optimized for high performance, making it suitable for applications where performance is crucial.

Cons:

• Less Familiarity: GetX might not be as widely adopted as other state management solutions.

These are just a few of the state management techniques available in Flutter. The choice of which to use depends on your specific project requirements and preferences. It's essential to evaluate the needs of your application and select the state management approach that best fits your use case.

Section 11.4: Streams and RxDart for

Reactive Programming

Reactive programming has gained popularity in Flutter app development due to its ability to handle asynchronous events and state changes efficiently. In this section, we'll explore the concept of streams and how the RxDart library can be used to implement reactive programming patterns in Flutter applications.

Understanding Streams

In Flutter, a **stream** is a sequence of asynchronous events. Streams are used to represent and handle data that is continuously flowing over time. They are especially useful for managing data that arrives incrementally, such as user input, sensor data, or data from network requests.

Creating a Stream

To create a stream, you can use the Stream class provided by Dart's core libraries. Here's a simple example of creating a stream of integers:

```
Stream<int> createCounterStream() async* {

for (int i = 1; i <= 10; i++) {

await Future.delayed(Duration(seconds: 1));

yield i;

}

}

final counterStream = createCounterStream();
```

In this example, createCounterStream() creates a stream that emits integers from 1 to 10 with a one-second delay between each emission.

Subscribing to a Stream

Once you have a stream, you can subscribe to it to receive its values. Flutter provides the StreamBuilder widget, which is commonly used to listen to and display the data emitted by a stream in the UI.

```
StreamBuilder<int>(

stream: counterStream,

builder: (context, snapshot) {

if (snapshot.connectionState == ConnectionState.waiting) {

return CircularProgressIndicator();

} else if (snapshot.hasError) {

return Text('Error: ${snapshot.error}');

} else {

return Text('Count: ${snapshot.data}');

}

},

)
```

In this example, the StreamBuilder widget listens to the counterStream and updates the UI whenever new data is emitted.

Introducing RxDart

RxDart is a popular Dart package that builds upon Dart's built-in streams to provide powerful tools for reactive programming. It offers a variety of stream operators and subjects for handling and manipulating data streams.

Key Concepts in RxDart

1. **Observable**: An Observable in RxDart represents a stream of data that can be observed. Observables are similar to streams but come with additional operators and methods.
2. **Subject**: A Subject is a special type of observable that can both produce and listen to data. RxDart provides various subject types, including BehaviorSubject, PublishSubject, and ReplaySubject, each with its unique characteristics.
3. **Operators**: RxDart offers a wide range of operators for transforming, filtering, combining, and manipulating data streams. Operators allow you to perform operations like map, filter, combineLatest, and more on your observables.

Using RxDart in Flutter

Here's an example of how to use RxDart in a Flutter application:

```
import 'package:rxdart/rxdart.dart';

void main() {

final subject = BehaviorSubject<int>();

subject.stream

.map((value) => value * 2)
```

```
.where((value) => value.isEven)
.listen((value) {
print('Received: $value');
});
subject.sink.add(1);
subject.sink.add(2);
subject.sink.add(3);
subject.close();
}
```

In this example, we create a BehaviorSubject named subject. We then chain operators on the subject.stream to map values, filter even values, and listen to the resulting stream. Finally, we add values to the subject.sink and close the subject when done.

RxDart provides a powerful set of tools for handling asynchronous data and state changes in Flutter applications. By leveraging streams and observables, you can build more responsive and interactive user interfaces, especially when dealing with real-time data and user interactions.

Section 11.5: Best Practices in State Management

Effective state management is crucial for building maintainable and performant Flutter applications. In this section, we'll discuss best practices and strategies for managing state in your Flutter apps.

1. Use Provider or Riverpod for Small to Medium-Sized Apps

For smaller to medium-sized Flutter applications, consider using the provider package or its modern variant, riverpod. These packages provide a simple and efficient way to manage and access state without the complexity of larger state management solutions. They are particularly well-suited for apps with a limited scope and fewer complex interactions.

2. Employ Bloc for Complex Logic

When dealing with complex business logic or larger applications, the Bloc (Business Logic Component) pattern, in combination with packages like flutter_bloc, can be an excellent choice. Bloc separates the UI from business logic and state management, making it easier to maintain and test your code.

3. Organize State into Models and Services

Keep your codebase clean and maintainable by organizing your application's state into models and services. Models represent the data structures and entities in your app, while services handle data retrieval, storage, and communication with external sources. This separation of concerns improves code readability and testability.

4. Minimize the Use of Global State

Avoid excessive reliance on global state. While global state management solutions like provider or riverpod offer convenience, overusing them can lead to a lack of clarity in your app's data flow. Instead, prefer local state management for UI-specific data and only use global state for essential app-wide data.

5. Leverage Immutable Data

Immutable data is easier to reason about and debug. When updating state, create new objects or data structures rather than modifying existing ones. Libraries like freezed or the copyWith method for classes with immutable properties can help achieve immutability.

6. Optimize Rebuilds with const Widgets

To minimize unnecessary widget rebuilds, use const widgets wherever possible. Const widgets are immutable and will not rebuild unless their properties change. This optimization can significantly improve app performance, especially in large and complex UIs.

```
Widget build(BuildContext context) {

return const Text('This is a constant widget');

}
```

7. Debounce User Input for Search and Filtering

When implementing search or filtering functionality, debounce user input to reduce the number of unnecessary network requests or computations. Packages like rxdart provide debounce operators that delay processing until the user has finished typing.

8. Implement State Restoration

For a seamless user experience, consider implementing state restoration. Flutter provides built-in support for preserving and restoring the state of widgets and screens, even across app restarts or device changes. This is especially important for mobile applications.

9. Profile and Optimize Performance

Regularly profile your Flutter app to identify performance bottlenecks. Tools like the Flutter DevTools can help you analyze frame rendering times, memory usage, and CPU performance. Optimize your code and UI to deliver a smooth user experience.

10. Stay Updated with Best Practices

Flutter and its ecosystem are continually evolving. Stay up-to-date with best practices and consider adopting new state management techniques and libraries as they become available. Active participation in the Flutter community can help you keep your skills sharp and your apps modern.

By following these best practices in state management, you can build Flutter applications that are not only robust and maintainable but also provide an excellent user experience. The right state management approach depends on your app's size and complexity, so choose the one that best suits your project's requirements.

Chapter 12: Asynchronous Programming in Dart

Section 12.1: The Role of Asynchrony in Modern Development

Asynchronous programming is a fundamental concept in modern software development. It enables applications to perform non-blocking operations, allowing tasks to be executed concurrently without freezing the user interface or causing delays. In Dart, asynchrony is achieved through the use of asynchronous functions and the async and await keywords. In this section, we will explore the significance of asynchrony and how it enhances the responsiveness and efficiency of Dart applications.

Understanding Blocking vs. Non-blocking Code

In traditional synchronous programming, operations are performed sequentially, one after the other. When an operation takes a significant amount of time to complete, it can block the entire application, making it unresponsive. For example, fetching data from a remote server synchronously could freeze the app until the data is received.

Asynchronous programming, on the other hand, allows the application to continue executing other tasks while waiting for time-consuming operations to complete. This non-blocking nature ensures that the app remains responsive and can handle multiple tasks simultaneously.

Use Cases for Asynchronous Programming

Asynchronous programming is essential in various scenarios:

1. **Network Requests:** When making HTTP requests or communicating with remote servers, it's crucial to do so asynchronously. This ensures that the UI remains responsive, and users can interact with the app while data is being fetched.
2. **File I/O:** Reading from or writing to files, especially large files, can be a time-consuming task. Asynchronous file operations prevent blocking the application.
3. **Database Access:** Interacting with databases often involves waiting for data retrieval or updates. Asynchronous database queries prevent UI freezes.
4. **User Input:** Handling user input asynchronously ensures that the app can process user actions without interruption.
5. **Animations:** Creating smooth animations often requires concurrent execution of multiple tasks. Asynchronous programming allows for seamless animations while other operations run in the background.

Dart's Asynchronous Model

Dart provides a straightforward model for handling asynchronous operations. Key components of Dart's asynchronous model include:

- **Future:** Represents a potential value or error that will be available at some point in the future. It allows you to initiate asynchronous operations and retrieve their results.

- **async/await:** The async and await keywords are used to define and wait for asynchronous operations within Dart functions. The async keyword indicates that a function is asynchronous, and await is used to pause the function's execution until a Future completes.

- **Completer:** A Completer is a way to create and control a Future manually. It allows you to complete a Future with a value or error explicitly.

In the upcoming sections of this chapter, we will delve deeper into Dart's asynchronous capabilities, explore common asynchronous patterns, and learn how to handle errors in asynchronous code.

Section 12.2: Working with Futures and Streams

In Dart, asynchronous programming revolves around two primary constructs: **Futures** and **Streams**. Understanding these concepts is crucial for effectively managing asynchronous operations and data flow within your application.

Futures

A **Future** in Dart represents a potential value or error that will be available at some point in the future. It is used to initiate and manage asynchronous operations. Futures are commonly used for tasks such as making network requests, reading files, or performing computations that may take time.

Here's a basic example of working with a Future in Dart:

```
Future<String> fetchData() async {

await Future.delayed(Duration(seconds: 2)); // Simulate a 2-second delay

return 'Data fetched successfully';

}
```

```
void main() {

print('Fetching data...');

fetchData().then((result) {

print(result); // This is executed when the Future completes

});

print('Data fetch initiated.');

}
```

In the code above, fetchData is an asynchronous function that simulates fetching data with a delay of 2 seconds. The await keyword is used to pause the function until the Future completes. The then method is used to register a callback that runs when the Future is resolved.

Streams

A **Stream** is a sequence of asynchronous events over time. Streams allow you to handle a continuous flow of data, making them suitable for real-time updates, event handling, and data streams like those from sensors, user input, or server-sent events.

Here's a basic example of working with a Stream in Dart:

```
import 'dart:async';

void main() {

final streamController = StreamController<int>();

final streamSubscription = streamController.stream.listen((data) {

print('Received data: $data');
```

```
});
streamController.sink.add(1);
streamController.sink.add(2);
streamController.sink.add(3);
streamSubscription.cancel(); // Cancel the subscription
streamController.close(); // Close the StreamController
}
```

In this example, we create a Stream using a StreamController. We then subscribe to the stream using listen to receive and handle incoming data. After adding three values to the stream, we cancel the subscription and close the StreamController to release resources.

Combining Futures and Streams

Futures and Streams can work together to handle asynchronous operations and data streams comprehensively. For example, you can convert a Stream into a Future using methods like first, last, or toList, allowing you to obtain a single value or a list of values from a Stream when it completes.

```
import 'dart:async';
Future<void> main() async {
final streamController = StreamController<int>();
streamController.sink.add(1);
streamController.sink.add(2);
streamController.sink.add(3);
```

```
final sum = await streamController.stream.reduce((acc, value) =>
acc + value);

print('Sum of values: $sum');

streamController.close();

}
```

In this example, we use the reduce method to calculate the sum of values in the Stream and await the result.

Understanding how to work with Futures and Streams is essential for developing responsive and efficient Dart applications, especially when dealing with asynchronous data and event-driven programming. In subsequent sections, we will explore advanced asynchronous patterns and techniques for handling more complex scenarios.

Section 12.3: Advanced Async Patterns and Techniques

In Dart, asynchronous programming often requires more than just using basic Futures and Streams. As applications grow in complexity, developers encounter scenarios where advanced patterns and techniques become necessary for efficient and maintainable code.

Future Combinators

Dart provides several combinators that make it easier to work with multiple Futures. These combinators allow you to perform operations like waiting for all Futures to complete, getting the first completed Future, or handling errors gracefully.

Future.wait

The Future.wait combinator is used to wait for a list of Futures to complete. It returns a Future that completes with a list of the individual results when all the input Futures have completed.

```
Future<void> main() async {

final futures = [

Future.delayed(Duration(seconds: 2), () => 'Result 1'),

Future.delayed(Duration(seconds: 1), () => 'Result 2'),

Future.delayed(Duration(seconds: 3), () => throw Exception('Error')),

];

try {

final results = await Future.wait(futures);

print('All results: $results');

} catch (e) {

print('An error occurred: $e');

}

}
```

In this example, we use Future.wait to wait for the list of Futures to complete. It will complete with an error if any of the input Futures throws an error.

Future.any

The Future.any combinator returns a Future that completes with the result of the first completed Future from a list of input Futures. This can be useful when you are interested in the first successful result.

```
Future<void> main() async {

final futures = [

Future.delayed(Duration(seconds: 2), () => 'Result 1'),

Future.delayed(Duration(seconds: 1), () => 'Result 2'),

Future.delayed(Duration(seconds: 3), () => 'Result 3'),

];

final result = await Future.any(futures);

print('First completed result: $result');

}
```

In this example, Future.any returns the first completed result, which is 'Result 2' in this case.

Streams Transformation

When working with Streams, you often need to transform or manipulate the data flowing through the stream. Dart provides a variety of Stream transformation methods to help with this.

map

The map method is used to transform each element of a Stream into a new value. It creates a new Stream with the transformed values.

```
import 'dart:async';

void main() {

final stream = Stream.fromIterable([1, 2, 3, 4, 5]);

final transformedStream = stream.map((value) => value * 2);

transformedStream.listen((value) {

print('Transformed value: $value');

});

}
```

In this example, we use map to create a new Stream that doubles each value in the original Stream.

where

The where method filters the elements of a Stream based on a condition and creates a new Stream containing only the elements that satisfy the condition.

```
import 'dart:async';

void main() {

final stream = Stream.fromIterable([1, 2, 3, 4, 5]);

final filteredStream = stream.where((value) => value.isEven);

filteredStream.listen((value) {

print('Even value: $value');

});
```

```
}
```

Here, where filters the original Stream to only include even numbers.

These are just a few examples of the advanced async patterns and techniques available in Dart. As you continue to work with asynchronous code in Dart, exploring and mastering these patterns will help you write more robust and efficient applications. In the following sections, we will delve into more advanced topics related to asynchronous programming in Dart.

Section 12.4: Error Handling in Asynchronous Code

Handling errors effectively is crucial in asynchronous code to ensure your application remains stable and can gracefully recover from unexpected issues. Dart provides mechanisms for handling errors in asynchronous code, including handling errors in Futures and Streams.

Handling Errors in Futures

When working with Futures, you can use the catchError method to handle errors that occur during asynchronous operations.

```
Future<void> main() async {

try {

final result = await fetchUserData();

print('User data: $result');

} catch (error) {

print('An error occurred: $error');
```

```
}
}
Future<String> fetchUserData() async {
await Future.delayed(Duration(seconds: 2));
throw Exception('Failed to fetch user data');
}
```

In this example, we have an asynchronous function fetchUserData that throws an error. We use a try-catch block to catch the error when awaiting the Future returned by fetchUserData. This allows us to handle the error gracefully.

You can also use the then method on a Future to specify a callback that will be invoked when the Future completes with an error.

```
Future<void> main() async {
fetchUserData()
.then((result) {
print('User data: $result');
})
.catchError((error) {
print('An error occurred: $error');
});
}
```

Handling Errors in Streams

When working with Streams, you can use the listen method to specify error handling logic.

```
void main() {

final stream = Stream<int>.error(Exception('Stream error'));

stream.listen(

(data) {

print('Received data: $data');

},

onError: (error) {

print('Error occurred: $error');

},

onDone: () {

print('Stream is done');

},

);

}
```

In this example, we create a Stream that emits an error, and we use the onError callback to handle the error when it occurs.

You can also use the async* generator function to create a Stream that yields values and handles errors.

```
Stream<int> generateStream() async* {
for (var i = 1; i <= 5; i++) {
yield i;
if (i == 3) {
throw Exception('Error at $i');
}
}
}
void main() {
generateStream()
.listen(
(data) {
print('Received data: $data');
},
onError: (error) {
print('Error occurred: $error');
},
onDone: () {
print('Stream is done');
},
```

```
);
}
```

In this example, the generateStream function generates values and throws an error when i equals 3. The onError callback handles the error.

Handling errors in asynchronous code is essential for building robust applications. Dart provides multiple mechanisms for error handling, enabling you to choose the one that best fits your needs and coding style.

Section 12.5: Practical Applications of Asynchronous Programming

Asynchronous programming is a powerful tool in Dart for handling tasks that would otherwise block your application's execution. In this section, we'll explore practical applications of asynchronous programming, demonstrating how it can improve the performance and responsiveness of your Dart applications.

1. Fetching Data from External Sources

One common use case for asynchronous programming is fetching data from external sources, such as APIs or databases. Using asynchronous operations allows your application to make network requests or database queries without freezing the user interface.

```
Future<void> fetchData() async {

final response = await http.get(Uri.parse('https://example.com/api/data'));

final data = json.decode(response.body);
```

```
// Process and display the data
}
```

Here, we use the http package to make an HTTP GET request to an API. The await keyword ensures that the network request is non-blocking and the application remains responsive.

2. Parallel Processing

Asynchronous programming allows you to perform multiple tasks concurrently, taking advantage of multi-core processors. For example, you can use Dart's Future.wait to execute multiple Futures in parallel.

```
Future<void> processImages(List<String> imageUrls) async {
final futures = imageUrls.map((url) => loadImage(url));
final images = await Future.wait(futures);
// Combine and display the processed images
}
```

In this example, we load multiple images concurrently, improving the overall processing time.

3. Timed Operations

Asynchronous programming is ideal for tasks that involve waiting for a specific amount of time, such as animations, timeouts, or periodic tasks.

```
Future<void> performAnimation() async {
for (var i = 0; i < 5; i++) {
```

```
await Future.delayed(Duration(seconds: 1));
// Update UI for animation frame i
}
}
```

By using Future.delayed, you can create timed animations or periodic updates without blocking the main thread.

4. Reactive Programming

Asynchronous programming is foundational for reactive programming, enabling applications to respond to data changes, user interactions, or external events in real-time.

```
final streamController = StreamController<int>();
void main() {
streamController.stream.listen((data) {
print('Received data: $data');
});
// Simulate data emission
for (var i = 1; i <= 5; i++) {
Future.delayed(Duration(seconds: i), () {
streamController.sink.add(i);
});
}
```

```
}
```

In this example, we create a StreamController to handle data streams and react to data changes asynchronously.

5. Concurrent I/O Operations

When working with files, databases, or other I/O-bound tasks, asynchronous programming is essential for maintaining application responsiveness.

```
Future<void> writeToDisk() async {

final file = File('data.txt');

await file.writeAsString('Hello, Dart!');

}
```

Here, we use the File class to write data to a file asynchronously, ensuring that the operation doesn't block the main thread.

These practical applications demonstrate how asynchronous programming can improve the performance and user experience of Dart applications by handling time-consuming tasks efficiently. Whether you're building web applications, mobile apps, or server-side solutions, mastering asynchronous programming is a valuable skill in Dart development.

Chapter 13: Design Patterns and Architecture

Section 13.1: Introduction to Design Patterns in Dart

Design patterns are fundamental solutions to common programming problems that developers encounter during software development. They provide a structured approach to solving specific challenges, making code more maintainable, reusable, and understandable. In this section, we will introduce the concept of design patterns in the context of Dart programming.

What Are Design Patterns?

Design patterns are proven solutions to recurring software design problems. They capture best practices, and by using them, developers can avoid reinventing the wheel and create more efficient and maintainable code. Design patterns can be categorized into three main types:

1. **Creational Patterns:** These patterns deal with object creation mechanisms, trying to create objects in a manner suitable to the situation. Examples include Singleton, Factory, and Builder patterns.
2. **Structural Patterns:** Structural patterns focus on class and object composition. They help in forming larger structures from individual parts, making them more flexible and efficient. Examples include Adapter, Decorator, and Facade patterns.
3. **Behavioral Patterns:** Behavioral patterns are concerned with communication between objects, defining the ways

they interact and distribute responsibilities. Examples include Observer, Strategy, and Command patterns.

Benefits of Using Design Patterns

Using design patterns in your Dart applications offers several advantages:

- **Reusability:** Design patterns promote code reuse, allowing you to apply proven solutions to similar problems across different projects.

- **Maintainability:** Patterns make your code more structured and easier to maintain, as they encapsulate specific functionality and separate concerns.

- **Scalability:** By following design patterns, your codebase can scale more easily as your application grows in complexity.

- **Readability:** Patterns provide a common language for developers to understand and communicate design decisions.

Applying Design Patterns in Dart

Dart, being an object-oriented language, lends itself well to the implementation of design patterns. To apply a design pattern in Dart, you'll typically use classes, interfaces, and other object-oriented features. Additionally, Dart's support for features like mixins and generics can be beneficial when implementing certain patterns.

Throughout the following sections in this chapter, we will explore various design patterns and demonstrate how to implement them in Dart. Understanding these patterns and knowing when to apply them will enhance your ability to write robust and maintainable Dart code.

In the subsequent sections, we will delve into specific design patterns, starting with creational patterns, which deal with object creation mechanisms. We will provide code examples and explanations to help you grasp the practical application of these patterns in Dart development.

Let's begin by exploring creational design patterns in Dart and how they can be used to create objects efficiently and effectively.

Section 13.2: Structural, Creational, and Behavioral Patterns

In the previous section, we introduced the concept of design patterns in Dart and their significance in software development. We classified design patterns into three main types: creational, structural, and behavioral. In this section, we will dive deeper into these categories to provide a broader understanding of the various design patterns you can apply in your Dart projects.

Creational Patterns

1. Singleton Pattern

The Singleton pattern ensures that a class has only one instance and provides a global point of access to that instance. This can be helpful when you want to restrict the instantiation of a class to a single object, such as a configuration manager or a connection pool.

```
class Singleton {

static Singleton _instance;
```

```
Singleton._(); // Private constructor

static Singleton get instance {

_instance ??= Singleton._(); // Create instance if it doesn't exist

return _instance;

}

}
```

2. Factory Method Pattern

The Factory Method pattern defines an interface for creating objects but lets subclasses alter the type of objects that will be created. It is useful when you need to create objects that belong to a family of classes.

```
abstract class Product {

void printDescription();

}

class ConcreteProductA implements Product {

@override

void printDescription() {

print("Product A");

}

}

class ConcreteProductB implements Product {
```

```
@override
void printDescription() {
print("Product B");
}
}
abstract class Creator {
Product factoryMethod();
}
class ConcreteCreatorA extends Creator {
@override
Product factoryMethod() {
return ConcreteProductA();
}
}
class ConcreteCreatorB extends Creator {
@override
Product factoryMethod() {
return ConcreteProductB();
}
}
```

3. Builder Pattern

The Builder pattern separates the construction of a complex object from its representation, allowing the same construction process to create different representations. This is useful when you want to create objects with many optional components.

```
class Product {

String partA;

String partB;

String partC;

Product();

}

abstract class Builder {

void buildPartA();

void buildPartB();

void buildPartC();

Product getResult();

}

class ConcreteBuilder extends Builder {

Product product = Product();

@override

void buildPartA() {
```

```
product.partA = "Part A";

}

@override

void buildPartB() {

product.partB = "Part B";

}

@override

void buildPartC() {

product.partC = "Part C";

}

@override

Product getResult() {

return product;

}

}
```

Structural Patterns

1. Adapter Pattern

The Adapter pattern allows the interface of an existing class to be used as another interface. It is often used to make existing classes work with others without modifying their source code.

```
class Adaptee {
void specificRequest() {
print("Adaptee's specific request");
}
}
abstract class Target {
void request();
}
class Adapter extends Target {
final Adaptee _adaptee;
Adapter(this._adaptee);
@override
void request() {
print("Adapter's request");
_adaptee.specificRequest();
}
}
```

2. Decorator Pattern

The Decorator pattern allows you to attach additional responsibilities to an object dynamically. It is a flexible alternative to subclassing for extending functionality.

```
abstract class Component {

void operation();

}

class ConcreteComponent implements Component {

@override

void operation() {

print("ConcreteComponent operation");

}

}

abstract class Decorator implements Component {

final Component component;

Decorator(this.component);

@override

void operation() {

component.operation();

}

}
```

```
class ConcreteDecoratorA extends Decorator {

ConcreteDecoratorA(Component component) : super(component);

void addedBehavior() {

print("Decorator A added behavior");

}

@override

void operation() {

super.operation();

addedBehavior();

}

}
```

Behavioral Patterns

1. Observer Pattern

The Observer pattern defines a one-to-many dependency between objects so that when one object changes state, all its dependents are notified and updated automatically.

```
class Subject {

final List<Observer> _observers = [];

void attach(Observer observer) {

_observers.add(observer);
```

```
}
void detach(Observer observer) {
_observers.remove(observer);
}
void notify() {
for (var observer in _observers) {
observer.update(this);
}
}
}
abstract class Observer {
void update(Subject subject);
}
class ConcreteObserver implements Observer {
@override
void update(Subject subject) {
print("Observer received an update from subject.");
}
}
```

2. Strategy Pattern

The Strategy pattern defines a family of algorithms, encapsulates each one, and makes them interchangeable. It allows the algorithm to vary independently from clients that use it.

abstract class Strategy {

void execute

Section 13.3: Implementing MVC and MVVM in Dart

In this section, we'll explore how to implement two popular architectural patterns, Model-View-Controller (MVC) and Model-View-ViewModel (MVVM), in Dart applications. These patterns provide a structured way to separate concerns, making your code more maintainable and testable.

Model-View-Controller (MVC)

Overview

MVC is a widely used architectural pattern that divides an application into three interconnected components: **Model**, **View**, and **Controller**. Here's a brief overview of each component:

- **Model**: Represents the application's data and business logic. It is responsible for retrieving and manipulating data, as well as notifying observers (typically views) about changes.

- **View**: Represents the user interface (UI) and displays the data from the model to the user. It listens for updates from the model and reflects changes in the UI.

- **Controller**: Acts as an intermediary between the model and view. It handles user input, processes it, and updates the model accordingly. Controllers also receive updates from the model and update the view.

Implementation

Let's look at a simple Dart example of MVC:

```
// Model

class CounterModel {

int _count = 0;

int get count => _count;

void increment() {

_count++;

}

}

// View

class CounterView {

void displayCount(int count) {

print('Count: $count');
```

```
}

}

// Controller

class CounterController {

final CounterModel _model;

final CounterView _view;

CounterController(this._model, this._view);

void incrementCounter() {

_model.increment();

_view.displayCount(_model.count);

}

}

void main() {

final model = CounterModel();

final view = CounterView();

final controller = CounterController(model, view);

controller.incrementCounter(); // This updates the count and displays it.

}
```

In this example, the CounterModel represents our data (the count value), the CounterView displays the count, and the

CounterController handles user interactions and updates the model and view accordingly.

Model-View-ViewModel (MVVM)

Overview

MVVM is another architectural pattern that separates an application into three components: **Model**, **View**, and **ViewModel**. It is commonly used in modern front-end development and is particularly suited for building reactive applications.

- **Model**: Same as in MVC, represents the application's data and business logic.
- **View**: Represents the UI and displays data to the user.
- **ViewModel**: Acts as a mediator between the model and view. It exposes the data and commands needed by the view and often contains presentation logic.

Implementation

Here's a simple Dart example of MVVM:

```
// Model

class CounterModel {

int _count = 0;

int get count => _count;

void increment() {
```

```
_count++;
}
}
// ViewModel
class CounterViewModel {
final CounterModel _model;
CounterViewModel(this._model);
int get count => _model.count;
void incrementCounter() {
_model.increment();
}
}
// View
class CounterView {
final CounterViewModel _viewModel;
CounterView(this._viewModel);
void displayCount() {
print('Count: ${_viewModel.count}');
}
}
```

```
void main() {

final model = CounterModel();

final viewModel = CounterViewModel(model);

final view = CounterView(viewModel);

viewModel.incrementCounter();

view.displayCount(); // This displays the count using the ViewModel.

}
```

In MVVM, the CounterViewModel acts as a bridge between the model and view. It exposes the count property and an incrementCounter method to the view, making it easier to manage the UI's state and logic.

Both MVC and MVVM have their advantages and are suitable for different scenarios. The choice between them depends on your application's requirements and your team's familiarity with the patterns.

Section 13.4: Dependency Injection and Inversion of Control

In this section, we will delve into the concepts of Dependency Injection (DI) and Inversion of Control (IoC) and how they can be applied in Dart for building scalable and maintainable applications. These concepts are essential in achieving loose coupling and facilitating testability in your code.

Understanding Dependency Injection (DI)

Dependency Injection is a software design pattern that aims to reduce the tight coupling between components in your application. It allows you to provide the dependencies required by a class from the outside rather than creating them within the class. This promotes reusability and makes your code more flexible.

In Dart, you can implement DI by passing dependencies as constructor parameters or using libraries like get_it or provider to manage dependencies and provide them when needed.

```
class Database {

// Database implementation

}

class UserRepository {

final Database _database;

UserRepository(this._database);

// UserRepository methods

}
```

In this example, the UserRepository class depends on the Database class. Instead of creating a Database instance within UserRepository, we pass it as a parameter through the constructor.

Exploring Inversion of Control (IoC)

Inversion of Control is a broader concept that encompasses Dependency Injection. It refers to the practice of letting external components or frameworks control the flow of your application.

IoC ensures that your application's high-level modules are decoupled from low-level implementations, promoting modularity and testability.

Dart developers often use IoC containers like get_it or frameworks like Flutter's Provider for IoC. These tools facilitate the management and retrieval of dependencies in your application.

Practical Benefits of DI and IoC

1. **Testability**: DI and IoC make it easy to substitute real dependencies with mock objects during testing. This allows you to isolate and test individual components of your application.
2. **Loose Coupling**: By injecting dependencies, you reduce the direct coupling between components. This makes it easier to change implementations or add new features without affecting existing code.
3. **Modularity**: IoC promotes modularity by breaking your application into smaller, reusable components. This makes codebases more manageable and maintainable.
4. **Scalability**: With DI and IoC, you can scale your application by adding or replacing components without major code changes.
5. **Configuration Management**: You can centralize the configuration of dependencies, making it easier to manage different configurations for development, testing, and production environments.

Using DI and IoC in Dart

To implement DI and IoC in Dart, you can choose from various libraries and frameworks that provide dependency injection and inversion of control containers. Some popular options include:

- **get_it**: A simple yet powerful DI library for Dart and Flutter.

- **provider**: A package provided by the Flutter team that facilitates IoC and DI in Flutter applications.

- **Custom Implementations**: You can also implement your own DI/IoC container if your project's requirements are specific and you prefer a custom solution.

Using these tools, you can effectively manage dependencies, achieve loose coupling, and create more maintainable Dart applications. The choice of which tool to use depends on your specific project needs and familiarity with the available options.

Section 13.5: Building Scalable Application Architecture

In this final section of Chapter 13, we will discuss the importance of building a scalable application architecture in Dart. Scalability is a crucial aspect of software development, especially for applications that need to handle increasing loads, user bases, or complex functionalities. We will explore best practices and techniques to design an architecture that can grow with your application's requirements.

Why Scalability Matters

Scalability is the ability of an application to handle an increasing workload while maintaining performance and responsiveness. Building a scalable architecture is essential because:

1. **Future-Proofing**: Scalable architectures ensure that your application can adapt and expand as your user base and feature set grow.
2. **Improved Performance**: Scalable systems can distribute workloads efficiently, leading to better performance even under heavy loads.
3. **Cost Efficiency**: Scalable architectures can be more cost-effective, as they allow you to use resources efficiently and avoid overprovisioning.
4. **Maintainability**: A well-structured architecture makes it easier to maintain and enhance your application over time.

Architectural Principles for Scalability

To build a scalable Dart application, consider the following architectural principles:

1. **Microservices Architecture**: Divide your application into smaller, independent microservices that can be developed, deployed, and scaled separately. This approach allows you to focus on individual components and optimize them for scalability.
2. **Load Balancing**: Implement load balancers to distribute incoming requests evenly across multiple instances of your application. This prevents overloading a single server and ensures high availability.
3. **Database Scaling**: Use database sharding, replication, or NoSQL databases designed for scalability to handle large

volumes of data.

4. **Caching**: Employ caching mechanisms to store frequently accessed data and reduce the load on your backend services.
5. **Asynchronous Processing**: Utilize asynchronous processing for tasks that can be deferred, such as background jobs or message processing. Dart's support for futures and isolates can be beneficial in this regard.
6. **Elastic Scaling**: Design your architecture to allow for elastic scaling, where resources can be automatically added or removed based on demand. Cloud platforms like Google Cloud, AWS, and Azure provide services for this purpose.
7. **Monitoring and Analytics**: Implement robust monitoring and analytics to gain insights into your application's performance and scalability bottlenecks. Tools like Prometheus and Grafana can be valuable for this.

Dart and Scalability

Dart is well-suited for building scalable applications, especially when combined with frameworks like Flutter for frontend development and Aqueduct for backend services. The language's support for asynchronous programming and its growing ecosystem of libraries and packages enable developers to implement scalable solutions.

```
// Example of asynchronous code in Dart

Future<void> fetchData() async {

// Simulate fetching data asynchronously

await Future.delayed(Duration(seconds: 2));

print('Data fetched successfully');
```

```
}
```

By embracing Dart's concurrency features, building scalable applications becomes more manageable. Additionally, integrating Dart with cloud services and deploying on scalable infrastructure can help you achieve the desired level of scalability.

In conclusion, building a scalable architecture is crucial for the long-term success of your Dart applications. It involves careful planning, adherence to architectural principles, and the use of appropriate tools and technologies. Scalability ensures that your application can handle growth and provide a seamless experience to users, making it a fundamental aspect of Dart application development.

Chapter 14: Network Programming in Dart

Section 14.1: Basics of Network Communication

In this section, we will delve into the fundamentals of network programming in Dart. Network communication is a crucial aspect of modern applications, enabling them to exchange data with servers, APIs, and other clients. Dart provides robust tools and libraries to facilitate network interactions, making it suitable for a wide range of networking tasks.

Understanding Network Communication

Network communication involves the exchange of data between two or more devices over a network, such as the internet. This communication can take various forms, including:

- **HTTP Requests**: Used for retrieving data from web servers, sending data to servers, or interacting with RESTful APIs.

- **WebSocket**: Provides full-duplex communication channels over a single TCP connection, enabling real-time, bidirectional communication.

- **Socket Programming**: Allows low-level network communication, often used for creating custom protocols or services.

Dart's Network Libraries

Dart offers several libraries and packages for network programming:

1. **http package**: This package provides functions for making HTTP requests and handling responses. It's commonly used for RESTful API interactions.
2. **dio package**: Built on top of the http package, dio simplifies working with RESTful APIs by providing a more convenient API and features like request cancellation and interceptors.
3. **web_socket_channel package**: This package allows you to create WebSocket clients and servers in Dart, facilitating real-time communication.

Making HTTP Requests

Let's start with a basic example of making an HTTP GET request using the http package:

```
import 'package:http/http.dart' as http;

Future<void> fetchData() async {

final response = await http.get(Uri.parse('https://api.example.com/
data'));

if (response.statusCode == 200) {

print('Data fetched successfully: ${response.body}');

} else {

print('Failed to fetch data. Status code: ${response.statusCode}');

}
```

```
}
```

In this example, we import the http package, make an asynchronous GET request to a URL, and handle the response accordingly.

WebSocket Communication

WebSocket is essential for real-time applications. Dart's web_socket_channel package makes it easy to establish WebSocket connections. Here's a simple example:

```
import 'package:web_socket_channel/io.dart';

void main() async {

final channel = IOWebSocketChannel.connect('wss://example.com/socket');

channel.sink.add('Hello, WebSocket!');

channel.stream.listen((message) {

print('Received: $message');

});

}
```

In this snippet, we import the web_socket_channel package, connect to a WebSocket server, send a message, and listen for incoming messages.

Network programming is a vast topic, and Dart's libraries provide a robust foundation for building various network-related features in your applications. Whether you're working on a web app, mobile app, or server-side application, Dart has the tools you need to handle network communication effectively.

Section 14.2: HTTP and Web Sockets in Dart

In this section, we will explore HTTP and WebSocket communication in Dart. These protocols are fundamental for web and network programming, enabling applications to interact with servers and exchange data in real-time.

HTTP Communication

Making HTTP Requests

Dart provides the http package, which simplifies making HTTP requests and handling responses. Here's how you can use it to perform a basic GET request:

```
import 'package:http/http.dart' as http;

Future<void> fetchData() async {

final response = await http.get(Uri.parse('https://api.example.com/
data'));

if (response.statusCode == 200) {

print('Data fetched successfully: ${response.body}');

} else {

print('Failed to fetch data. Status code: ${response.statusCode}');

}

}
```

In this example, we import the http package, make an asynchronous GET request to a URL, and handle the response accordingly. You can also use http.post(), http.put(), and http.delete() for other HTTP methods.

Sending Data in HTTP Requests

Often, you need to send data in the body of an HTTP request, such as when submitting a form or sending JSON data to a server. Here's an example of sending JSON data in a POST request:

```
import 'dart:convert';

import 'package:http/http.dart' as http;

Future<void> sendData(Map<String, dynamic> data) async {

final response = await http.post(

Uri.parse('https://api.example.com/submit-data'),

headers: {'Content-Type': 'application/json'},

body: jsonEncode(data),

);

if (response.statusCode == 200) {

print('Data sent successfully');

} else {

print('Failed to send data. Status code: ${response.statusCode}');

}

}
```

In this code, we use jsonEncode() to convert a Dart map into a JSON string and set the Content-Type header to indicate JSON data in the request body.

WebSocket Communication

WebSocket is crucial for building real-time applications, such as chat apps or live updates. Dart's web_socket_channel package simplifies WebSocket communication. Here's a simple example:

```
import 'package:web_socket_channel/io.dart';

void main() async {

final channel =
IOWebSocketChannel.connect('wss://example.com/socket');

channel.sink.add('Hello, WebSocket!');

channel.stream.listen((message) {

print('Received: $message');

});

}
```

In this code, we import the web_socket_channel package, connect to a WebSocket server, send a message using channel.sink.add(), and listen for incoming messages with channel.stream.listen().

WebSocket is ideal for applications that require bidirectional, real-time communication, as it allows the server and client to push data to each other without the need for continuous polling.

Understanding HTTP and WebSocket communication is essential for building modern web and network applications in Dart. The provided examples should give you a solid foundation to work with these protocols and integrate them into your projects as needed.

Section 14.3: Creating RESTful APIs with Dart

In this section, we will delve into creating RESTful APIs (Representational State Transfer Application Programming Interfaces) using Dart. RESTful APIs are a fundamental part of modern web development, allowing different systems to communicate over HTTP by following a set of conventions and principles.

What is RESTful API?

REST (Representational State Transfer) is an architectural style that uses HTTP requests to perform CRUD (Create, Read, Update, Delete) operations on resources. RESTful APIs are designed around these principles:

1. **Stateless**: Each request from a client to the server must contain all the information needed to understand and fulfill the request. The server should not store any client state between requests.
2. **Client-Server**: There should be a separation between the client (the user interface) and the server (the data storage and processing). This separation allows for independent development and scalability.
3. **Uniform Interface**: RESTful APIs should have a consistent and predictable interface. This is typically achieved through the use of standard HTTP methods (GET, POST, PUT, DELETE) and meaningful URLs.
4. **Resource-Based**: Resources, such as data objects or

services, should be identified by unique URLs. These URLs serve as endpoints for interacting with resources.
5. **Representation**: Resources can have multiple representations (e.g., JSON, XML, HTML), and clients can specify the desired representation in their requests.

Creating RESTful APIs with Dart

Dart provides libraries and frameworks that make it straightforward to create RESTful APIs. One popular choice is to use the shelf package, which is a minimal, low-level web framework for Dart.

Setting Up a RESTful API Server

To set up a RESTful API server with Dart and shelf, you first need to create a Dart project and add the necessary dependencies to your pubspec.yaml file:

```
dependencies:

shelf: ^1.0.0

shelf_router: ^1.0.0
```

Next, you can create your API server:

```
import 'dart:io';

import 'package:shelf/shelf.dart';

import 'package:shelf_router/shelf_router.dart';

void main() {

final app = Router();

// Define a route that returns a simple JSON response
```

```
app.get('/hello', (Request request) {
final response = Response.ok('{"message": "Hello, World!"}');
return response.change(headers: {'content-type': 'application/json'});
});
// Start the server
final server = await serve(app, 'localhost', 8080);
print('Server listening on port ${server.port}');
}
```

In this example, we import the shelf and shelf_router packages, define a simple /hello route that returns a JSON response, and start the server on localhost at port 8080.

This is just a basic example to get you started. You can expand your API by adding more routes, handling different HTTP methods, and integrating with a database to perform CRUD operations on resources.

Conclusion

Creating RESTful APIs with Dart is a crucial skill for building web applications and services. Dart's simplicity and the shelf package's flexibility make it a great choice for developing APIs that adhere to RESTful principles. In the next section, we will explore authentication and authorization strategies for securing your APIs.

Section 14.4: Authentication and Authorization Strategies

In this section, we will dive into the critical topics of authentication and authorization when working with RESTful APIs in Dart. These two concepts are fundamental for securing your API endpoints and ensuring that only authorized users can access certain resources or perform specific actions.

Authentication vs. Authorization

Before we proceed, it's essential to understand the distinction between authentication and authorization:

- **Authentication**: Authentication is the process of verifying the identity of a user, device, or application. It answers the question, "Who are you?" Authentication typically involves credentials such as usernames and passwords or authentication tokens. Once a user is authenticated, they are given a means of identifying themselves in subsequent requests.

- **Authorization**: Authorization, on the other hand, is the process of determining whether a user or application has permission to perform a specific action or access a particular resource. It answers the question, "Are you allowed to do this?" Authorization relies on roles, permissions, and policies to control access to resources and actions.

Implementing Authentication

To implement authentication in your Dart API, you can follow these general steps:

1. **User Registration and Login**: Create endpoints for user registration and login. During registration, users provide their credentials, which are securely stored in your database. When users log in, you verify their credentials and generate an authentication token.
2. **Authentication Tokens**: Use tokens like JSON Web Tokens (JWTs) to authenticate users. After successful login, provide a token that the client includes in subsequent requests. This token should be securely stored on the client side.
3. **Middleware**: Implement middleware that checks the validity of authentication tokens on each incoming request. If a token is valid, allow access to the requested resource; otherwise, return an authentication error.

Here's a simplified example of middleware for authentication:

```
Middleware authenticateMiddleware() {

return (Handler innerHandler) {

return (Request request) async {

final authToken = request.headers['authorization'];

if (isValidAuthToken(authToken)) {

return await innerHandler(request);

} else {

return Response.forbidden('Authentication failed');

}

};
```

```
};
}
```

Implementing Authorization

Authorization is typically role-based, where users or applications have specific roles (e.g., user, admin) that grant them certain permissions. To implement authorization in your Dart API, consider these steps:

1. **Define Roles and Permissions**: Clearly define the roles and permissions within your application. For example, an admin might have permission to delete records, while a regular user can only read them.
2. **Role Assignment**: Assign roles to users during registration or based on their actions within the application. Store this information in your database.
3. **Middleware**: Implement middleware that checks a user's role and permissions before allowing access to specific resources or actions. For example, an admin can access admin-only routes.

Here's a simplified example of role-based authorization middleware:

```
Middleware authorizeMiddleware(String role) {
return (Handler innerHandler) {
return (Request request) async {
final userRole = getUserRoleFromToken(request.headers['authorization']);
if (userRole == role) {
```

```
return await innerHandler(request);
} else {
return Response.forbidden('Authorization failed');
}
};
};
}
```

Conclusion

Authentication and authorization are critical aspects of building secure RESTful APIs. Implementing these strategies ensures that your API remains protected from unauthorized access and misuse. In the next section, we will explore best practices in network security to further enhance the security of your Dart APIs.

Section 14.5: Best Practices in Network Security

Ensuring the security of your Dart applications and RESTful APIs is of utmost importance, especially when they are accessible over the network. In this section, we'll discuss several best practices and techniques to enhance the security of your network communication.

1. Use HTTPS (TLS/SSL)

Always use HTTPS for network communication to encrypt data transmitted between the client and server. This encryption ensures that sensitive information, such as user credentials and personal data, remains confidential. You can obtain SSL/TLS certificates from trusted certificate authorities (CAs) to enable HTTPS on your server.

In Dart, you can make secure HTTP requests using the http package with the https scheme:

```
import 'package:http/http.dart' as http;

void fetchDataOverHttps() async {

final response = await http.get(Uri.https('example.com', '/api/data'));

if (response.statusCode == 200) {

// Process the response data.

} else {

// Handle errors.

}

}
```

2. Input Validation

Always validate and sanitize user input on the server side to prevent injection attacks, such as SQL injection and cross-site scripting (XSS). Use libraries and frameworks that provide input validation and parameterized queries for database interactions.

3. Authentication Tokens

When implementing authentication, use secure token-based systems like JSON Web Tokens (JWTs). Ensure that tokens have expiration times, and always verify token signatures to prevent token tampering.

4. Authorization

Implement role-based access control (RBAC) or attribute-based access control (ABAC) to manage permissions and ensure that users or applications only have access to resources and actions they are authorized to perform.

5. Rate Limiting

Implement rate limiting to prevent abuse of your APIs. Rate limiting restricts the number of requests a client can make within a specified timeframe. Libraries like shelf_ratelimiter in Dart can help with this.

```
import 'package:shelf_ratelimiter/shelf_ratelimiter.dart';

final app = Router()..add(createRateLimiter().handler);
```

6. Content Security Policy (CSP)

Use Content Security Policy headers to mitigate cross-site scripting (XSS) attacks by specifying which sources of content are allowed to be loaded by a web page. Implement a strict CSP that only allows trusted sources.

7. Cross-Origin Resource Sharing (CORS)

When building web applications, implement CORS policies to control which domains are allowed to make requests to your server. Define specific origins that are permitted to access your API.

8. Error Handling

Be cautious with error messages returned by your API. Avoid revealing sensitive information in error responses, and provide generic error messages to clients. Log detailed errors on the server for debugging purposes.

9. Regular Security Audits

Regularly conduct security audits and penetration testing of your Dart applications and APIs to identify vulnerabilities and weaknesses. Address any issues promptly.

10. Security Headers

Implement security headers like X-Content-Type-Options, X-Frame-Options, and X-XSS-Protection in your server responses to enhance security and prevent common web vulnerabilities.

By following these best practices and staying informed about evolving security threats, you can significantly reduce the risk of security breaches in your Dart applications and RESTful APIs. Prioritize security from the beginning and make it an integral part of your development process.

Chapter 15: Graphics and Animation in Dart

In this chapter, we will explore the world of graphics and animation in Dart. Graphics and animation play a crucial role in creating visually engaging and interactive applications, whether they are web, mobile, or desktop-based. Dart provides powerful libraries and tools for working with graphics and creating stunning animations.

Section 15.1: Drawing Basics with Canvas

Canvas is a fundamental element in HTML5 that allows you to draw and manipulate graphics directly in the web browser. Dart provides a convenient way to work with the HTML5 Canvas element, enabling you to create custom graphics, animations, and interactive visual elements.

To get started with canvas drawing in Dart, you need to have an HTML file with a <canvas> element:

```
<!DOCTYPE html>

<html>

<head>

<title>Canvas Drawing Example</title>

</head>

<body>

<canvas id="myCanvas" width="400" height="400"></canvas>

<script type="application/dart" src="main.dart"></script>

<script src="packages/browser/dart.js"></script>

</body>

</html>
```

In this example, we have an HTML file with a canvas element named "myCanvas." We also include a Dart script named "main.dart."

Now, let's create the Dart script (main.dart) to draw on the canvas:

```
import 'dart:html';

void main() {

final CanvasElement canvas = querySelector('#myCanvas');

final CanvasRenderingContext2D context =
canvas.getContext('2d');

// Draw a red rectangle

context.fillStyle = 'red';

context.fillRect(50, 50, 100, 100);

// Draw a blue circle

context.beginPath();

context.arc(200, 200, 50, 0, 2 * 3.14);

context.fillStyle = 'blue';

context.fill();

}
```

In this Dart script, we first get a reference to the canvas element and its 2D rendering context. We then draw a red rectangle and a blue circle on the canvas. This is a simple example, but you can create complex graphics and animations by manipulating the canvas context and using various drawing functions.

Canvas is a versatile tool for creating custom graphics, charts, games, and more in your Dart applications. In the subsequent sections of this chapter, we will delve deeper into advanced graphics and animation techniques using Dart.

Section 15.2: Creating Custom Graphics and Shapes

In this section, we will explore how to create custom graphics and shapes using Dart and the HTML5 Canvas element. Custom graphics are essential for designing unique visual elements, charts, diagrams, and game graphics. Dart provides the tools and libraries necessary to draw custom shapes and graphics with precision.

Basic Drawing Operations

To start drawing custom graphics, you'll need to understand some basic drawing operations:

1. **Paths:** Paths are sequences of lines or curves used to define the outline of a shape. You can create paths using the beginPath() method, move the drawing cursor with moveTo(), and draw lines or curves with lineTo(), arc(), and other methods.
2. **Styling:** You can set the stroke (outline) and fill (interior) styles for shapes. Use strokeStyle and fillStyle to define the stroke and fill colors. For example, context.strokeStyle = 'red'; sets the outline color to red.
3. **Line Styles:** Customize line styles with lineWidth, lineCap, and lineJoin properties. lineWidth controls the line thickness, while lineCap determines how line ends are styled (e.g., round or square). lineJoin defines how lines join at corners.
4. **Gradients and Patterns:** You can fill shapes with gradients or patterns using createLinearGradient(), createRadialGradient(), and createPattern() methods.

Here's a basic example of drawing custom shapes:

```
import 'dart:html';

void main() {

final CanvasElement canvas = querySelector('#myCanvas');

final CanvasRenderingContext2D context = canvas.getContext('2d');

// Draw a custom shape

context.beginPath();

context.moveTo(50, 50);

context.lineTo(150, 50);

context.lineTo(100, 150);

context.closePath(); // Connect the last point to the start point

context.fillStyle = 'blue';

context.fill(); // Fill the shape with blue

context.strokeStyle = 'red';

context.lineWidth = 2;

context.stroke(); // Outline the shape with a red border

}
```

In this example, we draw a custom triangle. We start by defining a path with beginPath(), move to the initial point, and use lineTo() to draw lines connecting the points. closePath() connects the last point to the starting point, closing the shape. Finally, we set the fill color to blue, the outline color to red, and draw the shape with fill() and stroke().

Advanced Custom Graphics

Dart and Canvas provide the flexibility to create more complex graphics, including curves, arcs, and Bezier curves. You can also transform and manipulate graphics using transformations like translation, rotation, scaling, and skewing.

Here's a brief overview of some advanced techniques:

1. **Bezier Curves:** Use quadraticCurveTo() and bezierCurveTo() to create quadratic and cubic Bezier curves, respectively. These are useful for drawing smooth curves.
2. **Arcs and Circles:** Draw circles and arcs using the arc() method. You can create pie charts, clock faces, and circular diagrams with ease.
3. **Transformations:** Apply transformations to graphics using methods like translate(), rotate(), scale(), and transform(). These transformations allow you to position and modify shapes dynamically.
4. **Clipping:** You can use clipping to restrict drawing to a specific area. This is helpful for creating masked effects and complex compositions.

Custom graphics open up a world of possibilities for creating interactive and visually appealing applications. Whether you're designing games, data visualizations, or artistic displays, Dart and Canvas give you the tools to bring your ideas to life. In the next section, we'll explore animation principles and how to incorporate animations into your custom graphics.

Section 15.3: Animation Principles in Dart

Animation is a fundamental aspect of creating engaging and interactive user interfaces and games. In this section, we'll delve into animation principles and how to implement animations in Dart applications. Understanding animation basics is crucial for bringing life to your custom graphics and creating dynamic user experiences.

The Animation Loop

Animations typically involve a continuous loop where frames are rendered sequentially, creating the illusion of motion. In Dart, you can implement this animation loop using techniques like requestAnimationFrame() or the Timer class. The key idea is to update the animation state and redraw the scene in each frame.

Here's a simple example of an animation loop using requestAnimationFrame():

```
import 'dart:html';

void main() {

final CanvasElement canvas = querySelector('#myCanvas');

final CanvasRenderingContext2D context = canvas.getContext('2d');

num angle = 0;

void drawFrame(num highResTime) {

angle += 0.01; // Update animation state

context.clearRect(0, 0, canvas.width, canvas.height); // Clear the canvas
```

```
drawRotatingSquare(context, angle); // Draw the animated object

window.requestAnimationFrame(drawFrame); // Request the next frame

}

void drawRotatingSquare(CanvasRenderingContext2D context, num angle) {

final size = 50;

final centerX = canvas.width / 2;

final centerY = canvas.height / 2;

context.save(); // Save the current context state

context.translate(centerX, centerY); // Translate to the center

context.rotate(angle); // Rotate

context.fillStyle = 'blue';

context.fillRect(-size / 2, -size / 2, size, size); // Draw a square

context.restore(); // Restore the context state

}

window.requestAnimationFrame(drawFrame); // Start the animation loop

}
```

In this example, we continuously rotate a square using the animation loop. We update the angle variable in each frame, clear the canvas, draw the square, and request the next frame. This creates a smooth rotation effect.

Easing Functions

To add more realism to animations, you can apply easing functions. Easing functions control the rate of change of a value over time, allowing you to create effects like acceleration and deceleration. Dart offers libraries like easing_functions to easily incorporate easing into your animations.

```
import 'package:easing_functions/easing_functions.dart';

// Example of using an easing function

final easeOutQuad = EasingFunctions.easeOutQuad;

final initialValue = 0.0;

final targetValue = 100.0;

final duration = const Duration(seconds: 1);

final currentTime = const Duration(milliseconds: 500);

final animatedValue = initialValue + (targetValue - initialValue) * easeOutQuad(currentTime.inMilliseconds / duration.inMilliseconds);
```

Easing functions come in various types, such as linear, quadratic, cubic, and more. You can experiment with different easing functions to achieve the desired animation effects.

Frame Rate and Performance

Consider the frame rate (frames per second, or FPS) when designing animations. Lower frame rates may result in choppy animations, while higher frame rates can be demanding on system resources. Aim for a balance between smoothness and performance, typically targeting 60 FPS.

To optimize performance, minimize the number of objects being redrawn and use techniques like double buffering to prevent flickering.

In summary, animation in Dart involves creating an animation loop, updating animation states in each frame, and redrawing the scene. Easing functions add realism to animations, and you should aim for an appropriate frame rate for smooth and performant animations. In the next section, we'll explore interactive graphics and user interfaces.

Section 15.4: Interactive Graphics and User Interfaces

Creating interactive graphics and user interfaces (UI) is a core part of many Dart applications. Whether you're developing games, data visualization tools, or complex web applications, building responsive and interactive UI elements is crucial for a positive user experience. In this section, we'll explore techniques for implementing interactive graphics and UI in Dart.

Event Handling

Event handling is the foundation of interactivity in Dart applications. Dart provides an event-driven model for responding to user actions, such as clicks, mouse movements, and keyboard input. You can attach event listeners to HTML elements and handle events using Dart code.

Here's an example of handling a button click event:

```
import 'dart:html';

void main() {

final ButtonElement button = querySelector('#myButton');

final DivElement output = querySelector('#output');

button.onClick.listen((MouseEvent event) {

output.text = 'Button clicked!';

});

}
```

In this example, we select an HTML button element and a div element by their IDs and attach a click event listener to the button. When the button is clicked, the text in the output div is updated to indicate the click event.

Canvas Graphics

For more advanced graphics and animations, the HTML5 <canvas> element is commonly used. You can draw shapes, images, and custom graphics on a canvas element using Dart's CanvasRenderingContext2D API. This allows you to create interactive games, data visualizations, and other dynamic content.

```
import 'dart:html';

void main() {

final CanvasElement canvas = querySelector('#myCanvas');

final CanvasRenderingContext2D context =
canvas.getContext('2d');
```

```
canvas.onClick.listen((MouseEvent event) {

context.fillStyle = 'blue';

context.fillRect(50, 50, 100, 100);

});

}
```

In this example, we create a canvas element and attach a click event listener. When the canvas is clicked, a blue rectangle is drawn on it using the fillRect() method.

User Interface Libraries

To simplify UI development, you can use Dart libraries and frameworks that provide pre-designed UI components and widgets. One popular option is the Flutter framework, which allows you to build natively compiled applications for mobile, web, and desktop from a single codebase. Flutter provides a rich set of customizable UI widgets and handles user interaction seamlessly.

Another option is the dart:ui library, which offers a set of basic UI components and can be used to build custom UI elements from scratch.

Responsiveness and Layout

Creating responsive UI is essential to ensure your applications work well on various screen sizes and orientations. Dart provides tools for responsive design, such as media queries, flex layouts, and responsive UI libraries. These techniques help adapt your UI to different devices and screen resolutions.

In summary, interactivity and UI design are crucial aspects of Dart application development. Event handling, canvas graphics, and the use of UI libraries are key techniques for creating engaging user experiences. Additionally, ensuring responsiveness and adaptability to different devices is essential for modern applications. Next, we'll explore integrating 3D graphics using WebGL.

Section 15.5: Integrating 3D Graphics with WebGL

Integrating 3D graphics into your Dart applications can add a new dimension of visual appeal and interactivity. WebGL, a web standard for rendering 3D graphics in web browsers, can be used alongside Dart to create stunning 3D visuals and interactive experiences. In this section, we'll explore how to integrate 3D graphics with WebGL in Dart applications.

What is WebGL?

WebGL (Web Graphics Library) is a JavaScript API that allows web developers to access and utilize the GPU (Graphics Processing Unit) for rendering 3D graphics within web browsers. It brings the power of 3D graphics to web applications without requiring additional plugins or installations. WebGL is based on OpenGL ES (Embedded Systems), a widely-used 3D graphics API.

Using WebGL with Dart

To use WebGL in your Dart applications, you can leverage the dart:web_gl package, which provides Dart bindings for WebGL. This package allows you to create and manage WebGL contexts, shaders, buffers, textures, and other essential components for 3D rendering.

Here's a basic example of setting up a WebGL context in Dart:

```
import 'dart:html';

import 'dart:web_gl' as gl;

void main() {

final CanvasElement canvas = querySelector('#myCanvas');

final gl.RenderingContext context = canvas.getContext('webgl');

if (context == null) {

print('WebGL is not supported.');

return;

}

// Now you can start using WebGL for 3D rendering.

}
```

In this example, we obtain a WebGL context from an HTML canvas element. If WebGL is not supported in the user's browser, we display a message indicating that WebGL is not available.

Creating 3D Scenes

Once you have a WebGL context set up, you can create 3D scenes by defining geometries, materials, lights, and cameras. WebGL provides APIs for rendering 3D objects and applying textures, shaders, and animations. Libraries like Three.js, which has Dart bindings, can simplify the process of creating complex 3D scenes.

Here's a basic example of rendering a cube in a WebGL scene using Three.js in Dart:

```
import 'dart:html';

import 'dart:web_gl' as gl;

import 'package:three/three.dart';

void main() {

final CanvasElement canvas = querySelector('#myCanvas');

final gl.RenderingContext context = canvas.getContext('webgl');

if (context == null) {

print('WebGL is not supported.');

return;

}

final scene = Scene();

final camera = PerspectiveCamera(75, 1, 0.1, 1000);

final renderer = WebGLRenderer(context: context, canvas: canvas);

final geometry = BoxGeometry(1, 1, 1);

final material = MeshBasicMaterial(color: 0x00ff00);

final cube = Mesh(geometry, material);

camera.position.z = 5;

scene.add(cube);

final animate = (num time) {

window.requestAnimationFrame(animate);
```

```
cube.rotation.x += 0.01;

cube.rotation.y += 0.01;

renderer.render(scene, camera);

};

animate(0);

}
```

In this example, we create a rotating cube in a Three.js scene and render it using WebGL.

WebGL Considerations

While WebGL offers powerful capabilities for 3D graphics, it's essential to consider performance and compatibility. Not all devices and browsers fully support WebGL, and rendering complex 3D scenes can be resource-intensive. Therefore, optimizing your WebGL code and providing fallbacks for non-supported platforms is crucial.

In summary, integrating 3D graphics with WebGL in Dart applications opens up possibilities for creating immersive and interactive visual experiences. By leveraging the dart:web_gl package and libraries like Three.js, you can harness the full potential of WebGL for your projects. However, be mindful of performance considerations and provide graceful degradation for users on non-supported platforms.

Chapter 16: Dart for IoT and Embedded Systems

In this chapter, we delve into the exciting world of IoT (Internet of Things) and embedded systems with Dart. IoT is a rapidly growing field that involves connecting physical devices to the internet to collect and exchange data. Dart, with its versatility and performance, is a suitable choice for developing applications on IoT devices and embedded systems. We'll explore various aspects of using Dart in this domain.

Section 16.1: Introduction to IoT with Dart

IoT represents a paradigm shift in computing, where everyday objects are equipped with sensors, actuators, and connectivity to enhance their functionality. In this section, we introduce the fundamentals of IoT and its relevance to Dart. We'll discuss the key components of IoT systems, the role of Dart in this ecosystem, and the unique challenges and opportunities presented by IoT development.

Section 16.2: Dart on Embedded Systems

Embedded systems are specialized computing devices with dedicated functions, ranging from microcontrollers in household appliances to industrial automation systems. Dart's suitability for embedded systems is driven by its efficient execution, low memory footprint, and compatibility with hardware. In this section, we explore the concepts of embedded systems and how Dart can be deployed on them.

Section 16.3: Building IoT Applications with

Dart

Building IoT applications involves connecting sensors, processing data, and controlling actuators. Dart's support for asynchronous programming, combined with libraries like dart:io and dart:ffi, makes it a powerful choice for developing IoT applications. In this section, we dive into practical examples of developing IoT applications with Dart.

Section 16.4: Communication Protocols and Hardware Integration

IoT devices communicate with each other and with central servers using various communication protocols. Dart supports popular IoT communication protocols, such as MQTT and CoAP, making it easier to build interconnected IoT systems. We'll also discuss hardware integration and the use of GPIO (General-Purpose Input/ Output) pins for controlling sensors and actuators.

Section 16.5: Case Studies: Dart in IoT Projects

To provide a real-world perspective, we present case studies of IoT projects developed using Dart. These case studies demonstrate how Dart can be applied to create practical IoT solutions, ranging from home automation and environmental monitoring to industrial IoT applications.

By the end of this chapter, you'll have a solid understanding of how Dart can be used effectively in IoT and embedded systems development, and you'll be equipped with the knowledge to embark on your own IoT projects using Dart.

Chapter 16: Dart for IoT and Embedded Systems

Section 16.1: Introduction to IoT with Dart

The Internet of Things (IoT) is a revolutionary technology that has gained immense popularity in recent years. It involves connecting physical objects, devices, and machines to the internet to collect and exchange data, enabling them to interact with the physical world and other connected devices. IoT has applications in various domains, including smart homes, healthcare, industrial automation, agriculture, and more.

IoT Fundamentals

At its core, IoT comprises three main components:

1. **Devices/Things:** These are the physical objects or devices equipped with sensors, actuators, and communication modules. Examples include temperature sensors, smart thermostats, wearable fitness trackers, and industrial machines.
2. **Connectivity:** IoT devices need a way to connect to the internet or other devices. This can be achieved through various communication protocols, such as Wi-Fi, Bluetooth, Zigbee, LoRa, cellular networks, or even satellite communication.
3. **Cloud Services and Applications:** Data collected from IoT devices is typically sent to cloud servers for storage, processing, and analysis. Mobile or web applications can access this data and provide user interfaces for control and monitoring.

Dart's Role in IoT

Dart, known for its versatility and performance, is well-suited for developing applications for IoT devices and embedded systems. Here's why Dart is a strong contender in this domain:

- **Efficiency:** Dart's Ahead-of-Time (AOT) compilation and efficient execution make it suitable for resource-constrained IoT devices with limited processing power and memory.

- **Concurrency:** IoT applications often require handling multiple concurrent tasks, such as reading sensor data and sending it to the cloud. Dart's asynchronous programming model, built on top of Futures and Streams, simplifies handling concurrency.

- **Platform Support:** Dart supports various platforms, including ARM-based devices commonly used in IoT and embedded systems. It's versatile enough to run on microcontrollers, single-board computers (SBCs), and more.

- **Libraries:** Dart provides libraries for network communication (dart:io), serial communication (dart:ffi), and interaction with GPIO pins, which are essential for IoT development.

- **Safety:** Dart's strong type system and null safety features enhance code reliability, a crucial factor for mission-critical IoT applications.

- **Community and Ecosystem:** Dart benefits from a growing community and third-party packages that extend its capabilities, making it easier to build IoT solutions.

Challenges and Opportunities

While Dart has many advantages for IoT development, there are challenges to consider:

- **Hardware Diversity:** IoT encompasses a wide range of devices with varying hardware capabilities. Developers must choose the right hardware platform and peripherals for their specific application.

- **Power Efficiency:** IoT devices often run on battery power or have strict power requirements. Optimizing code for power efficiency is crucial for extending battery life.

- **Security:** IoT devices are susceptible to security threats. Dart developers must be well-versed in security best practices to protect sensitive data and prevent unauthorized access.

- **Interoperability:** IoT devices may need to communicate with devices using different protocols or standards. Dart's support for various communication protocols is essential for interoperability.

In this chapter, we'll explore how Dart can be used effectively in IoT and embedded systems development. We'll delve into practical examples, case studies, and best practices to equip you with the knowledge and skills needed to create IoT solutions using Dart. Whether you're interested in building a smart home automation system, monitoring industrial equipment, or developing wearable devices, Dart can be your go-to language for IoT development.

Section 16.2: Dart on Embedded Systems

Dart's versatility extends beyond just web and mobile applications; it's also a viable choice for developing applications on embedded systems. Embedded systems are specialized computing systems designed for specific tasks or functions, often with limited hardware resources. Dart's lightweight nature, efficient resource management, and portability make it a compelling option for embedded system development.

Dart on Embedded Platforms

Dart can be used on various embedded platforms, including but not limited to:

1. **Single-Board Computers (SBCs):** SBCs like Raspberry Pi, BeagleBone, and Arduino can run Dart applications. These boards are versatile and provide GPIO pins, making them suitable for a wide range of projects.
2. **Microcontrollers:** Dart can be used on microcontrollers, especially those supported by the Dart dart:ffi (Foreign Function Interface) library. Microcontrollers power countless IoT devices and embedded systems.
3. **Custom Hardware:** In cases where custom hardware is involved, Dart can be adapted to the specific needs of the project. Dart's open-source nature allows developers to customize the language and runtime to fit their requirements.

Advantages of Using Dart on Embedded Systems

1. Portability: Dart's cross-platform compatibility allows developers to write code that runs on various embedded platforms without significant modifications. This reduces development time and effort.

2. Performance: Dart's efficient execution and memory management make it suitable for resource-constrained environments. Dart applications on embedded systems can be optimized for speed and responsiveness.

3. Concurrency: Dart's asynchronous programming model, based on Futures and Streams, simplifies handling concurrent tasks commonly encountered in embedded systems, such as sensor data reading and event handling.

4. Community and Libraries: Dart benefits from an active developer community and a growing ecosystem of packages. Developers can leverage existing libraries for tasks like network communication, sensor interfacing, and more.

5. Safety: Dart's strong type system and optional null safety features enhance code reliability, crucial for embedded systems where errors can have serious consequences.

Use Cases for Dart in Embedded Systems

Dart can be used in various embedded system applications, including:

- **Home Automation:** Building smart home systems that control lighting, heating, and security devices.

• **Industrial Control:** Monitoring and controlling machinery and equipment in industrial settings.

• **IoT Gateways:** Developing gateways that connect IoT devices to the cloud.

• **Consumer Electronics:** Creating custom applications for embedded devices in consumer electronics products.

• **Robotics:** Building control software for robots and automation systems.

• **Healthcare Devices:** Developing software for medical devices and wearables.

Dart's Limitations in Embedded Systems

While Dart has numerous advantages for embedded systems, there are certain limitations to consider:

1. **Limited Ecosystem:** The Dart ecosystem for embedded systems is smaller compared to languages like C/C++ or Rust, which have been traditionally used in this domain.
2. **Resource Management:** Developers need to be mindful of resource usage, especially on microcontrollers with tight constraints.
3. **Interoperability:** Dart's interoperability with hardware-specific features may require additional effort and expertise.

In conclusion, Dart's flexibility, portability, and performance make it a promising language for embedded systems and IoT development. As we explore further in this chapter, we'll delve into practical examples and demonstrate how to harness Dart's potential for various embedded platforms and applications.

Section 16.3: Building IoT Applications with Dart

Building Internet of Things (IoT) applications with Dart is an exciting endeavor that leverages the language's strengths in resource efficiency, portability, and asynchronous programming. IoT involves connecting physical devices and sensors to the internet, enabling them to collect and exchange data, and facilitating remote control and monitoring. Dart's versatility makes it suitable for a wide range of IoT use cases, from smart home automation to industrial IoT solutions.

Key Components of IoT Applications

Before delving into building IoT applications with Dart, it's essential to understand the key components involved:

1. **IoT Devices:** These are physical devices or sensors equipped with computing capabilities and communication interfaces. Examples include temperature sensors, cameras, and smart thermostats.
2. **Connectivity:** IoT devices connect to the internet using various protocols like Wi-Fi, Bluetooth, Zigbee, or cellular networks. This connectivity enables data transmission to and from the devices.
3. **Cloud Services:** Data from IoT devices is typically sent to cloud-based servers or platforms for storage, processing, and analysis. Cloud services can provide real-time data processing, remote control, and data visualization.
4. **User Interfaces:** Web or mobile applications serve as

interfaces for users to interact with IoT devices and access data. Dart can be used to build these user interfaces.

Developing IoT Applications with Dart

1. Device Programming: Dart can be used to program IoT devices directly, especially if they have the capability to run Dart code. For microcontrollers, Dart's dart:ffi library can be used to interface with device-specific libraries and APIs.

2. Server-Side Logic: Dart is well-suited for implementing server-side logic in IoT applications. Developers can create server applications that handle device communication, data storage, and real-time processing using Dart and frameworks like Aqueduct or Shelf.

3. Web and Mobile Interfaces: Dart can be used to build web and mobile applications that interact with IoT devices. For web development, Dart can be compiled to JavaScript to create responsive and user-friendly web interfaces. In mobile app development, Flutter with Dart is an excellent choice for cross-platform IoT applications.

Example IoT Use Cases with Dart

Here are some examples of IoT use cases that can be developed using Dart:

- **Smart Home Automation:** Control and monitor lighting, thermostats, security cameras, and appliances from a mobile app or web interface.

- **Environmental Monitoring:** Use Dart to program IoT devices that collect data on air quality, temperature, humidity, and more, then visualize this data through a web dashboard.

- **Industrial IoT (IIoT):** Implement real-time monitoring and predictive maintenance solutions for industrial equipment and machinery using Dart on both IoT devices and cloud servers.

- **Healthcare IoT:** Create wearable devices and healthcare sensors that transmit patient data to medical professionals via secure Dart-powered applications.

- **Agricultural IoT:** Develop IoT solutions for precision agriculture, including soil moisture monitoring, automated irrigation, and crop health analysis.

Challenges and Considerations

While Dart offers many advantages for IoT development, there are some challenges and considerations to keep in mind:

- **Resource Constraints:** IoT devices often have limited processing power and memory. Dart applications need to be optimized for resource efficiency.

- **Security:** IoT applications must prioritize security to protect sensitive data and prevent unauthorized access to devices.

- **Interoperability:** Ensure that Dart-based IoT devices can communicate with other devices and services through standardized protocols.

In this section, we will explore practical examples of building IoT applications with Dart and discuss best practices for addressing these challenges effectively.

Section 16.4: Communication Protocols and Hardware Integration

In the context of IoT applications with Dart, communication protocols play a vital role in enabling devices to transmit data reliably and efficiently. Additionally, hardware integration is crucial for interfacing with sensors, actuators, and other physical components. This section explores common communication protocols and hardware integration techniques when building IoT applications with Dart.

Communication Protocols

1. **MQTT (Message Queuing Telemetry Transport):** MQTT is a lightweight publish-subscribe protocol ideal for IoT. Dart provides the mqtt_client package, allowing you to connect to MQTT brokers, publish messages, and subscribe to topics. MQTT is well-suited for scenarios where low bandwidth and minimal overhead are essential.
2. **CoAP (Constrained Application Protocol):** CoAP is designed for constrained devices and low-power networks. Dart offers the coap package, enabling you to create CoAP clients and servers. It's suitable for resource-constrained IoT environments.
3. **HTTP and Web Sockets:** Dart supports HTTP and WebSocket communication, making it versatile for connecting IoT devices to web services or cloud platforms. You can use the http package for HTTP requests and the web_socket_channel package for WebSocket

communication.

4. **Bluetooth:** For IoT applications that involve Bluetooth connectivity, Dart provides the flutter_blue package, which simplifies communication with Bluetooth Low Energy (BLE) devices. This is especially useful for building mobile apps that interact with IoT devices.

Hardware Integration

1. **GPIO (General-Purpose Input/Output):** Dart can interface with GPIO pins on devices like Raspberry Pi using libraries like dart_io or rpi_gpio. This enables control of LEDs, relays, and sensors.
2. **Serial Communication:** To communicate with devices using serial protocols like UART, Dart offers the serial_port package. It's handy for connecting to microcontrollers and other embedded systems.
3. **I2C and SPI:** If your IoT devices use I2C or SPI communication, Dart libraries such as i2c and spi can be used to interact with sensors and peripherals that rely on these protocols.
4. **Sensor Libraries:** Dart provides packages for various sensors, such as the dht package for DHT temperature and humidity sensors. These libraries simplify reading data from sensors and integrating it into your IoT applications.
5. **Modbus and PLC Communication:** For industrial IoT applications, Dart can communicate with programmable logic controllers (PLCs) using the modbus package, enabling control and monitoring of industrial processes.

Example: MQTT Communication with Dart

```
import 'package:mqtt_client/mqtt_client.dart';
```

```
import 'package:mqtt_client/mqtt_server_client.dart';

Future<void> main() async {

final client = MqttServerClient('mqtt.eclipse.org', '');

client.logging(on: true);

await client.connect();

if (client.connectionStatus!.state == MqttConnectionState.connected) {

print('Connected to MQTT broker');

client.subscribe('topic/sensors', MqttQos.atMostOnce);

client.updates.listen((List<MqttReceivedMessage<MqttMessage>>? event) {

final MqttPublishMessage payload = event![0].payload as MqttPublishMessage;

final message = MqttPublishPayload.bytesToStringAsString(

payload.payload.message,

);

print('Received message: $message');

});

final builder = MqttClientPayloadBuilder();

builder.addString('Hello from Dart MQTT client');

client.publishMessage('topic/sensors', MqttQos.atMostOnce, builder.payload!);
```

```
// Disconnect when done

await Future.delayed(const Duration(seconds: 10));

await client.disconnect();

print('Disconnected from MQTT broker');

} else {

print(

'Failed to connect to MQTT broker - '

'Is the broker running or the network reachable?',

);

}

}
```

In this example, Dart connects to an MQTT broker, subscribes to a topic, and publishes a message. This demonstrates how Dart can be used to establish IoT communication using MQTT.

This section has provided an overview of communication protocols and hardware integration techniques with Dart in IoT applications. Depending on your specific IoT project requirements, you can choose the most appropriate protocols and libraries for your use case.

Section 16.5: Case Studies: Dart in IoT Projects

To gain a deeper understanding of how Dart is applied in real-world Internet of Things (IoT) projects, let's explore a few case studies that highlight its versatility and effectiveness in addressing IoT challenges.

Case Study 1: Smart Home Automation

In this project, Dart is used to build a smart home automation system. The system includes various IoT devices like smart lights, thermostats, and security cameras. Dart is employed for both mobile app development and backend server implementation.

- **Mobile App Development:** Flutter, powered by Dart, is the go-to choice for building cross-platform mobile apps. The smart home mobile app allows users to control and monitor devices remotely. It provides a responsive and intuitive user interface.

- **Backend Server:** Dart is used to develop a backend server that facilitates communication between the mobile app and IoT devices. The server handles user authentication, device control commands, and real-time data synchronization.

Case Study 2: Industrial Monitoring and Control

In this industrial IoT project, Dart is utilized to create a monitoring and control system for a manufacturing plant. The system connects to various sensors, programmable logic controllers (PLCs), and actuators on the factory floor.

- **Communication:** Dart's support for MQTT and Modbus communication protocols is crucial. MQTT is used for real-time data streaming, while Modbus is employed for control commands. Dart libraries simplify the integration of these protocols.

- **Data Visualization:** The project uses Dart libraries to visualize data from sensors and devices in real-time. Graphs and charts display production statistics and machine statuses, aiding plant operators in decision-making.

Case Study 3: Environmental Monitoring

In this environmental monitoring application, Dart is chosen for its efficiency and compatibility with resource-constrained IoT devices. The project involves deploying IoT sensors to gather data on air quality, temperature, and humidity in urban areas.

- **Low-Power Devices:** Dart's support for low-power IoT devices is crucial in this project. It ensures that sensors can operate on battery power for extended periods without frequent replacements.

- **Data Collection:** Dart libraries enable the IoT devices to collect data and transmit it to a central server using CoAP, a lightweight IoT protocol. The server processes the data and provides real-time air quality information to the public through a web application.

Case Study 4: Agriculture and Precision Farming

In the agriculture sector, Dart is applied to enhance precision farming techniques. IoT sensors and drones equipped with Dart-based applications are used to monitor soil conditions, crop health, and irrigation needs.

- **Drone Control:** Dart is used to develop drone control software, enabling autonomous flight, image capture, and data analysis. Drones equipped with cameras and sensors fly over fields, capturing images and gathering data.

- **Data Analytics:** Dart's capabilities in data processing and analysis are harnessed to interpret data from sensors and drone images. Machine learning models are employed to predict crop yields and optimize irrigation strategies.

These case studies demonstrate the versatility of Dart in a wide range of IoT applications, from smart homes to industrial monitoring, environmental sensing, and precision agriculture. Dart's capabilities in mobile app development, backend server creation, and efficient communication make it a valuable choice for IoT projects that require both versatility and performance.

Chapter 17: Dart for Server-Side Development

Section 17.1: Setting Up a Dart Server

Dart has evolved beyond a language just for front-end development and mobile apps; it's now a capable choice for server-side development as well. In this section, we'll delve into setting up a Dart server for web applications, APIs, and more.

Dart's Server-Side Strengths

Before we dive into the setup, let's highlight some of the strengths that make Dart an excellent choice for server-side development:

1. **Performance:** Dart boasts a highly optimized virtual machine that delivers impressive server-side performance. It competes well with other server-side languages like

Node.js, Python, and Ruby.

2. **Single Language:** If you're already using Dart for front-end development (e.g., with Flutter), you can leverage the same language and libraries for the back end. This reduces the learning curve and ensures consistency in your codebase.
3. **Asynchronous Programming:** Dart excels in handling asynchronous operations, making it well-suited for handling multiple concurrent connections efficiently. Asynchronous programming is crucial for server-side development, where waiting for I/O operations can be a bottleneck.
4. **Strong Typing:** Dart's strong type system helps catch errors at compile-time, reducing the likelihood of runtime errors in your server-side code.

Setting Up Dart for Server-Side

To get started with Dart for server-side development, you'll need to follow these steps:

1. **Install Dart:** If you haven't already, install Dart on your development machine. You can download it from the official Dart website (https://dart.dev/).
2. **Choose a Server Framework:** Dart provides several server frameworks to choose from. Two popular options are Aqueduct and Shelf. Aqueduct is a full-featured framework for building RESTful APIs, while Shelf is a minimalist framework that gives you more control over the architecture.
3. **Create a Dart Project:** Use the dart create command to create a new Dart project for your server-side application.

This will set up the project structure and configuration files.

4. **Define Routes and Handlers:** Depending on your chosen framework, define routes and request handlers for your server. This is where you specify how incoming HTTP requests should be processed.
5. **Implement Business Logic:** Write the business logic for your server application. This could involve database interactions, authentication, data processing, and more.
6. **Testing and Deployment:** Thoroughly test your server application to ensure it works as expected. Once satisfied, deploy it to your chosen hosting environment. Dart servers can be deployed on various platforms, including cloud services like Google Cloud, AWS, or on your own servers.
7. **Monitoring and Maintenance:** After deployment, set up monitoring to keep an eye on your server's performance and stability. Regularly maintain and update your server-side code to address security vulnerabilities and add new features.

Example Code (Using Shelf):

Here's a simplified example of setting up a basic HTTP server using the Shelf framework:

```
import 'package:shelf/shelf.dart';

import 'package:shelf/shelf_io.dart' as shelf_io;

void main() async {

final handler = const Pipeline()

.addMiddleware(logRequests()) // Middleware for logging requests
```

```
.addHandler(_handleRequest);

final server = await shelf_io.serve(handler, 'localhost', 8080);

print('Server running on ${server.address}:${server.port}');

}

Response _handleRequest(Request request) {

return Response.ok('Hello, Dart Server!');

}
```

This code creates a simple Dart HTTP server that responds with "Hello, Dart Server!" to incoming requests. It uses the Shelf framework, which is known for its simplicity and flexibility.

In the subsequent sections of this chapter, we will explore more advanced topics related to Dart for server-side development, including building web servers and APIs, working with middleware, and optimizing server performance.

Section 17.2: Building Web Servers and APIs

In the previous section, we discussed setting up a Dart server and briefly introduced the concept of routing and request handling. In this section, we'll dive deeper into building web servers and APIs using Dart.

Creating a Simple Web Server

To create a basic web server in Dart, we can use the Shelf framework, which provides a straightforward way to handle HTTP requests and responses. Here's a step-by-step guide to building a simple web server:

1. **Add Shelf Dependency:** If you haven't already, add the Shelf dependency to your Dart project's pubspec.yaml file.

```
dependencies:

shelf: ^1.0.0
```

Run pub get to fetch the dependencies.

1. **Import the Required Libraries:**

```
import 'package:shelf/shelf.dart';

import 'package:shelf/shelf_io.dart' as shelf_io;
```

1. **Create a Request Handler:**

```
Response _handleRequest(Request request) {

return Response.ok('Hello, Dart Web Server!');

}
```

In this example, _handleRequest is a function that handles incoming HTTP requests and responds with "Hello, Dart Web Server!".

1. **Set Up the Server:**

```
void main() async {

final handler = const Pipeline()

.addMiddleware(logRequests()) // Middleware for logging requests
```

```
.addHandler(_handleRequest);

final server = await shelf_io.serve(handler, 'localhost', 8080);

print('Server running on ${server.address}:${server.port}');

}
```

This code sets up the server and specifies the request handler. It also includes middleware for logging incoming requests.

1. **Run the Server:**

Run your Dart program, and you should see the server running on localhost at port 8080. You can access it by opening a web browser or using tools like curl or httpie.

Routing and Handling Multiple Endpoints

In real-world applications, you'll likely need to define multiple endpoints and handle different types of requests (e.g., GET, POST, PUT, DELETE). Shelf makes this easy with its routing mechanism.

Here's a brief example of how to define routes and handle different HTTP methods:

```
Response _handleGet(Request request) {

return Response.ok('This is a GET request.');

}

Response _handlePost(Request request) {
```

```
return Response.ok('This is a POST request.');

}

void main() async {

final cascade = Cascade()

.add((Request request) {

if (request.method == 'GET') {

return _handleGet(request);

}

if (request.method == 'POST') {

return _handlePost(request);

}

return Response.notFound('Endpoint not found.');

});

final server = await shelf_io.serve(cascade.handler, 'localhost', 8080);

print('Server running on ${server.address}:${server.port}');

}
```

In this example, we've defined separate functions for handling GET and POST requests, and we use the Cascade class to route requests based on their HTTP method.

Building RESTful APIs

To create a RESTful API, you can follow similar principles but define routes for various resources and map them to appropriate request handlers. Additionally, you'll need to handle request payloads, query parameters, and authentication, depending on your API's requirements.

In the subsequent sections of this chapter, we will explore more advanced topics related to Dart server-side development, including working with middleware, scalability, and real-world case studies of Dart in server-side applications.

Section 17.3: Working with Middleware in Dart

Middleware is a crucial concept in web development, and it plays a significant role in the Dart ecosystem as well. Middleware functions intercept and process HTTP requests and responses before they reach the main request handler. This allows you to add common functionalities such as logging, authentication, error handling, and more to your web server or API without cluttering your request handling code. In this section, we'll explore working with middleware in Dart.

Adding Middleware to Your Dart Server

Dart web frameworks like Shelf make it easy to work with middleware. Let's take an example of how to add logging middleware to a Dart web server built with Shelf:

```
import 'package:shelf/shelf.dart';

import 'package:shelf/shelf_io.dart' as shelf_io;
```

```
import 'package:shelf_logger/shelf_logger.dart';

Response _handleRequest(Request request) {

return Response.ok('Hello, Dart Web Server!');

}

void main() async {

final handler = const Pipeline()

.addMiddleware(logRequests()) // Logging middleware

.addHandler(_handleRequest);

final server = await shelf_io.serve(handler, 'localhost', 8080);

print('Server running on ${server.address}:${server.port}');

}
```

In this example, we've added the logRequests() middleware using the addMiddleware method of the Pipeline class. This middleware logs incoming requests, including details like the request method, URI, and response status.

Creating Custom Middleware

While there are pre-built middleware libraries available for common use cases, you can also create your custom middleware functions. Custom middleware functions should have the signature (Handler) -> Handler, which means they take a request handler as input and return a new request handler.

Here's a simple example of custom middleware that adds a custom header to every response:

```
Handler addCustomHeaderMiddleware(String headerName, String headerValue) {

return (Handler innerHandler) {

return (Request request) async {

final response = await innerHandler(request);

return response.change(headers: {

headerName: headerValue,

});

};

};

}
```

You can use this custom middleware as follows:

```
final handler = const Pipeline()

.addMiddleware(addCustomHeaderMiddleware('X-Custom-Header', 'MyValue'))

.addHandler(_handleRequest);
```

This middleware will add the X-Custom-Header header with the value MyValue to every response.

Middleware for Authentication and Authorization

Middleware is often used to implement authentication and authorization in web applications. You can create middleware that checks authentication tokens or session cookies and verifies user permissions before allowing access to certain routes or resources. Building authentication middleware is a complex topic and typically involves integrating with authentication providers or databases.

In summary, middleware in Dart provides a flexible way to add functionality to your web servers and APIs. Whether you need to log requests, implement authentication, handle errors, or perform any other tasks, Dart's middleware ecosystem has you covered. It allows you to keep your code modular and maintainable by separating concerns and reusing middleware across different parts of your application.

Section 17.4: Scalability and Performance Optimization

Scalability and performance are critical aspects of server-side development, and Dart offers several techniques and tools to help you optimize your Dart web applications for better scalability and performance. In this section, we'll explore some best practices and strategies for making your Dart server applications performant and scalable.

1. Asynchronous Programming

Dart's asynchronous programming model is essential for building high-performance servers. By leveraging asynchronous operations with Futures and Streams, you can handle multiple requests concurrently without blocking the event loop. Make sure to use asynchronous libraries and functions whenever possible, especially when dealing with I/O-bound operations like file or database access.

```
Future<void> fetchData() async {

// Simulating an asynchronous operation
```

```
await Future.delayed(Duration(seconds: 1));

print('Data fetched!');

}
```

2. Connection Pooling

When working with databases or external services, connection pooling can significantly improve performance. Dart's database packages often provide connection pooling mechanisms that allow you to reuse database connections across multiple requests instead of opening a new connection for each request. This reduces overhead and improves response times.

```
final pool = PostgreSQLConnectionPool(

'localhost',

5432,

'my_database',

username: 'user',

password: 'password',

max: 5, // Maximum connections in the pool

);
```

3. Caching

Caching frequently used data or responses can reduce the load on your server and improve response times. Dart offers caching libraries like cache and moor that you can integrate into your server applications to store and retrieve cached data efficiently.

```
final cache = Cache<String, dynamic>();

Future<dynamic> fetchData(String key) async {

return cache.getOrCompute(key, () async {

// Fetch data from the source if not found in the cache

return fetchDataFromSource(key);

});

}
```

4. Load Balancing

To distribute incoming traffic evenly and ensure high availability, consider using load balancing techniques. Dart server applications can be deployed in clusters behind load balancers, such as Nginx or HAProxy, which distribute incoming requests to multiple server instances. This prevents a single server from becoming a bottleneck and improves both scalability and fault tolerance.

5. Profiling and Monitoring

Regularly monitor and profile your Dart server applications to identify performance bottlenecks and optimize code. Tools like the Dart Observatory, logging, and third-party monitoring solutions can help you gain insights into application performance, memory usage, and request processing times.

6. Proper Error Handling

Efficient error handling is crucial for maintaining server performance. Handle errors gracefully and avoid throwing exceptions for expected conditions. Use Dart's error handling mechanisms, such as try-catch blocks, to handle errors without causing crashes.

```
try {
// Code that may throw an exception
} catch (e) {
// Handle the error
print('An error occurred: $e');
}
```

7. Caching Responses

For responses that don't change frequently, consider implementing caching mechanisms on the client side using HTTP caching headers like Cache-Control and ETag. This can reduce the number of requests your server needs to handle and improve client-side performance.

In conclusion, optimizing the performance and scalability of your Dart server applications requires a combination of asynchronous programming, connection pooling, caching, load balancing, profiling, and proper error handling. By following these best practices and considering the specific needs of your application, you can build high-performance and scalable Dart server applications that meet the demands of your users.

Section 17.5: Case Studies: Dart in Server-Side Applications

In this section, we'll explore real-world case studies of how Dart has been successfully used in server-side applications. These examples showcase the versatility and capabilities of Dart in various domains.

1. Aqueduct Framework for RESTful APIs

Dart Aqueduct[5] is a modern, high-performance web framework for building RESTful APIs. It leverages Dart's strengths in asynchronous programming and is well-suited for developing backend services. With built-in support for authentication, database integration, and validation, Aqueduct simplifies the development of robust server applications.

```
import 'package:aqueduct/aqueduct.dart';

class UserController extends ResourceController {

UserController(this.context);

final ManagedContext context;

@Operation.get()

Future<Response> getAllUsers() async {

final query = Query<User>(context);

final users = await query.fetch();

return Response.ok(users);

}
```

5. https://aqueduct.io/

}

2. Shelf: A Lightweight Middleware Framework

Dart Shelf is a minimalistic, composable middleware framework that allows developers to build custom server applications. It's particularly well-suited for small to medium-sized projects where simplicity and flexibility are key.

```
import 'package:shelf/shelf.dart';

import 'package:shelf/shelf_io.dart' as io;

Response helloHandler(Request request) {

return Response.ok('Hello, Dart Shelf!');

}

void main() {

final handler = const Pipeline()

.addMiddleware(logRequests())

.addHandler(helloHandler);

io.serve(handler, 'localhost', 8080).then((server) {

print('Serving at http://${server.address.host}:${server.port}');

});

}
```

3. Fuchsia Operating System

Dart is a core component of Google's experimental Fuchsia operating system[6]. Fuchsia demonstrates Dart's adaptability to system-level programming and its ability to power various components of an operating system, including the user interface, device drivers, and more.

4. Firebase Functions for Serverless Computing

Firebase, Google's mobile and web application development platform, allows developers to write serverless functions using Dart. These functions can respond to events from Firebase services or HTTP requests. Dart's fast startup times and efficient execution make it a great choice for serverless computing.

```
import 'package:firebase_functions/firebase_functions.dart';

Future<void> main() async {

final function = FirebaseFunctions.instance.httpsCallable('myFunction');

final result = await function.call({'param1': 'value1', 'param2': 'value2'});

print('Function result: ${result.data}');

}
```

5. Angel Framework for Full-Stack Development

Angel[7] is a full-stack Dart framework for building web, mobile, and backend applications. It provides a wide range of features, including

6. https://fuchsia.dev/

7. https://angel-dart.dev/

routing, dependency injection, authentication, and database integration. Angel showcases Dart's capabilities for building end-to-end applications.

```
import 'package:angel_framework/angel_framework.dart';

import 'package:angel_framework/http.dart';

main() async {

final app = Angel();

app.get('/', (req, res) => res.write('Hello, Angel Dart!'));

await AngelHttp(app).startServer('localhost', 3000);

}
```

These case studies illustrate the diverse range of applications where Dart has proven to be a valuable choice for server-side development. Whether you're building RESTful APIs, serverless functions, operating systems, or full-stack applications, Dart's performance and versatility make it a compelling option for a variety of server-side use cases.

Chapter 18: Dart and Machine Learning

Section 18.1: Introduction to Machine Learning in Dart

Machine Learning (ML) has become a transformative technology with applications in various domains, from natural language processing to computer vision and recommendation systems. In this section, we'll explore how Dart, a language known for its versatility and performance, can be used in the context of machine learning.

The Role of Machine Learning

Machine Learning is a subfield of artificial intelligence that focuses on developing algorithms and models that enable computers to learn and make predictions or decisions based on data. It has gained immense popularity due to its ability to analyze large datasets and extract valuable insights.

Machine learning can be broadly categorized into three types:

1. **Supervised Learning:** This involves training a model using labeled data, where the input and corresponding output are known. The model learns to map inputs to outputs and can make predictions on new, unseen data.
2. **Unsupervised Learning:** In this type, the model works with unlabeled data and tries to find patterns or structure within the data. Common techniques include clustering and dimensionality reduction.
3. **Reinforcement Learning:** This area focuses on training agents to interact with an environment and learn from

feedback or rewards. It has applications in robotics and game playing.

Dart and Machine Learning

Dart, as a versatile and performant language, has gained recognition in the field of machine learning. While it may not be as widely adopted as languages like Python or R in the machine learning community, Dart offers several advantages:

- **Performance:** Dart's performance is comparable to languages like C++ and Java, making it suitable for computationally intensive ML tasks.

- **Concurrency:** Dart's asynchronous programming capabilities are beneficial for handling concurrent tasks, which is essential in many ML applications.

- **Flutter Integration:** If you're building mobile or web applications with Flutter, using Dart for machine learning ensures consistency in your tech stack.

- **Cross-Platform:** Dart is a cross-platform language, which means you can develop machine learning models that work seamlessly on different operating systems.

- **Libraries:** While Dart's ML ecosystem is not as extensive as Python's, there are libraries and packages available for tasks like data manipulation, neural networks, and data visualization.

To use Dart effectively in machine learning, you'll typically leverage existing libraries or connect with ML frameworks. TensorFlow, for example, provides a Dart package that allows you to integrate TensorFlow models into your Dart applications.

In the upcoming sections, we'll dive deeper into Dart's role in machine learning, exploring data processing, model integration, and real-world applications. Whether you're a Dart enthusiast or looking for a performant language for ML tasks, this chapter will provide valuable insights into the intersection of Dart and machine learning.

Section 18.2: Data Processing and Analysis

In the field of machine learning, data processing and analysis are crucial steps that lay the foundation for building effective models. In this section, we'll explore how Dart can be used for data manipulation, cleaning, and analysis in the context of machine learning projects.

Data Preprocessing

Before feeding data into machine learning models, it's essential to preprocess it to ensure its quality and suitability for training. Dart provides various libraries and tools to help with data preprocessing tasks.

Data Loading

Dart allows you to read and load data from various sources, such as CSV files, databases, and web APIs. You can use the csv package to parse CSV files, the http package for web API requests, and other packages for specific data sources.

```
import 'dart:io';

import 'package:csv/csv.dart';
```

```
void main() async {
final input = File('data.csv').readAsStringSync();
final rows = const CsvToListConverter().convert(input);
print(rows);
}
```

Data Cleaning

Cleaning data involves handling missing values, outliers, and inconsistencies. Dart's standard libraries provide functions for filtering and transforming data efficiently. You can also use libraries like dataframe for more advanced data manipulation.

```
import 'package:dataframe/dataframe.dart';
void main() {
final data = DataFrame.fromMap({
'A': [1, 2, 3, 4, null],
'B': [5, 6, 7, 8, 9],
});
final cleanedData = data.dropNull(); // Remove rows with null values
print(cleanedData);
}
```

Exploratory Data Analysis (EDA)

EDA is the process of visually and statistically analyzing data to discover patterns, relationships, and insights. Dart can be used to create visualizations and perform statistical analysis on your data.

Data Visualization

Dart provides libraries like charts_flutter that allow you to create various types of charts and graphs to visualize your data.

```
import 'package:charts_flutter/flutter.dart' as charts;

void main() {

final data = [

SalesData('Jan', 100),

SalesData('Feb', 200),

SalesData('Mar', 150),

// ...

];

final series = [

charts.Series<SalesData, String>(

id: 'Sales',

data: data,

domainFn: (SalesData sales, _) => sales.month,

measureFn: (SalesData sales, _) => sales.amount,
```

```
),
];
final chart = charts.BarChart(
series,
animate: true,
);
// Display the chart
}
```

Statistical Analysis

Dart also provides mathematical libraries for performing statistical analysis, hypothesis testing, and data summary statistics.

```
import 'package:statistics/statistics.dart';
void main() {
final data = [1, 2, 3, 4, 5];
final mean = mean(data);
final variance = variance(data);
final correlation = correlation(data, data);
print('Mean: $mean');
print('Variance: $variance');
print('Correlation: $correlation');
```

```
}
```

Data Transformation

In some cases, you may need to transform data to create new features or preprocess it for specific algorithms. Dart provides the tools to perform these transformations efficiently.

```
void main() {

final data = [1, 2, 3, 4, 5];

final transformedData = data.map((value) => value * 2).toList();

print(transformedData); // [2, 4, 6, 8, 10]

}
```

Conclusion

Data processing and analysis are fundamental aspects of any machine learning project. Dart, with its libraries and tools, can be a reliable choice for these tasks. Whether you're loading data, cleaning it, visualizing patterns, or transforming features, Dart provides the flexibility and performance needed for effective data preparation in machine learning projects. In the next section, we'll delve into integrating Dart with machine learning frameworks and building predictive models.

Section 18.3: Integrating Dart with ML Frameworks

Integrating Dart with machine learning (ML) frameworks is essential for building, training, and deploying ML models effectively. In this section, we'll explore how Dart can be used alongside popular

ML frameworks to create predictive models and perform data analysis.

TensorFlow and TFLite

TensorFlow is one of the most popular ML frameworks, and Dart has bindings to TensorFlow through the tflite package. These bindings allow you to load pre-trained TensorFlow models and perform inference directly from your Dart applications.

```
import 'package:tflite/tflite.dart';

void main() async {

// Load a pre-trained TensorFlow Lite model

await Tflite.loadModel(

model: 'assets/model.tflite',

labels: 'assets/labels.txt',

);

// Perform inference on an input image

final output = await Tflite.runModelOnImage(

path: 'assets/input.jpg',

);

print(output);

}
```

MLKit

MLKit is a suite of machine learning tools provided by Google, and it can be used in Dart applications through the firebase_ml_vision package. MLKit offers features like image recognition, text recognition, and language identification.

```
import 'package:firebase_ml_vision/firebase_ml_vision.dart';

void main() async {

final FirebaseVisionImage visionImage = FirebaseVisionImage.fromFilePath('path/to/image.jpg');

final TextRecognizer textRecognizer = FirebaseVision.instance.textRecognizer();

final VisionText visionText = await textRecognizer.processImage(visionImage);

for (TextBlock block in visionText.blocks) {

for (TextLine line in block.lines) {

for (TextElement element in line.elements) {

print(element.text);

}

}

}

textRecognizer.close();

}
```

Dart Libraries for Machine Learning

While Dart may not have as many ML libraries as some other languages, it is continually evolving. Dart libraries like ml_linalg and ml_algo provide the fundamental building blocks for creating custom machine learning models from scratch.

```
import 'package:ml_linalg/linalg.dart';

import 'package:ml_algo/ml_algo.dart';

void main() {

final data = [

[1, 2, 3, 4, 5],

[2, 3, 4, 5, 6],

// ...

];

final labels = [0, 1, 0, 1, 0];

final classifier = LogisticRegressor(

optimizerType: GD(),

numberOfIterations: 1000,

);

final model = classifier.fit(Matrix.fromList(data), labels);

final predictions = model.predict(Matrix.fromList(data));

print(predictions);
```

```
}
```

Python Integration

Another approach to leverage the power of Python-based ML libraries is by using the dart:ffi library for Foreign Function Interface (FFI) to call Python code from Dart. This allows you to utilize libraries like scikit-learn and TensorFlow, which have well-established Python APIs.

```
import 'dart:ffi' as ffi;

void main() {

final python = ffi.DynamicLibrary.open('libpython3.so'); // Load Python library

final initializePython = python

.lookupFunction<ffi.Void Function(), void Function()>(

'Py_Initialize',

);

initializePython(); // Initialize Python interpreter

// Call Python code here

final finalizePython = python

.lookupFunction<ffi.Void Function(), void Function()>(

'Py_Finalize',

);

finalizePython(); // Finalize Python interpreter
```

}

Conclusion

Integrating Dart with machine learning frameworks is essential for building predictive models and performing data analysis. Whether you choose TensorFlow, MLKit, Dart libraries, or even Python integration, Dart provides the flexibility and tools needed to work seamlessly with various machine learning technologies. In the next section, we'll explore building predictive models in Dart and showcase real-world applications of Dart in machine learning.

Section 18.4: Building Predictive Models in Dart

Building predictive models is a fundamental aspect of machine learning, and Dart provides the necessary tools and libraries to create and train these models. In this section, we'll delve into building predictive models in Dart, covering key concepts and practical examples.

Data Preparation

Before building predictive models, it's crucial to prepare and preprocess your data. Dart offers libraries like ml_linalg and ml_preprocessing that assist in data manipulation, transformation, and cleaning.

```
import 'package:ml_linalg/linalg.dart';

import 'package:ml_preprocessing/ml_preprocessing.dart';

void main() {

// Sample data
```

```
final data = [
[1.0, 2.0, 3.0],
[4.0, 5.0, 6.0],
// ...
];
// Create a matrix from the data
final matrix = Matrix.fromList(data);
// Standardize the data
final scaler = StandardScaler();
final scaledData = scaler.fit(matrix).transform(matrix);
print(scaledData);
}
```

Supervised Learning

Supervised learning is a common approach for building predictive models where the algorithm learns from labeled data. Dart provides libraries like ml_algo that offer various algorithms for regression and classification tasks.

```
import 'package:ml_algo/ml_algo.dart';
import 'package:ml_linalg/linalg.dart';
void main() {
// Sample data
```

```
final data = [
[1.0, 2.0],
[2.0, 3.0],
[3.0, 4.0],
// ...
];
final labels = [0.0, 1.0, 0.0, // ...
// Create a classifier
final classifier = LogisticRegressor(
optimizerType: GD(),
numberOfIterations: 1000,
);
// Fit the model
final model = classifier.fit(Matrix.fromList(data), labels);
// Make predictions
final predictions = model.predict(Matrix.fromList(data));
print(predictions);
}
```

Unsupervised Learning

Unsupervised learning involves discovering patterns or structures in data without labeled outcomes. Dart offers libraries like ml_cluster for clustering and ml_anomaly_detection for anomaly detection.

```
import 'package:ml_cluster/ml_cluster.dart';

import 'package:ml_linalg/linalg.dart';

void main() {

// Sample data

final data = [

[1.0, 2.0],

[2.0, 3.0],

[3.0, 4.0],

// ...

];

// Create a k-means clustering model

final kmeans = KMeans(

k: 2,

iterations: 100,

);

// Fit the model

final clusters = kmeans.fit(Matrix.fromList(data));
```

```
print(clusters);

}
```

Evaluating Models

Evaluating the performance of your predictive models is crucial. Dart libraries like ml_metrics offer metrics for assessing model accuracy, precision, recall, and other evaluation measures.

```
import 'package:ml_metrics/ml_metrics.dart';

void main() {

final actualLabels = [1, 0, 1, 0, 1];

final predictedLabels = [1, 0, 0, 0, 1];

final accuracy = accuracyScore(actualLabels, predictedLabels);

final precision = precisionScore(actualLabels, predictedLabels);

final recall = recallScore(actualLabels, predictedLabels);

print('Accuracy: $accuracy');

print('Precision: $precision');

print('Recall: $recall');

}
```

Deployment

Once you've built and evaluated your predictive models, you can deploy them in Dart applications to make real-time predictions or integrate them into larger systems.

In conclusion, Dart provides a range of libraries and tools for building predictive models, whether for supervised or unsupervised learning tasks. Understanding data preparation, selecting appropriate algorithms, and evaluating model performance are key steps in the machine learning workflow. In the next section, we'll explore real-world applications of Dart in machine learning, showcasing how Dart can be used to solve practical problems.

Section 18.5: Real-World Applications of Dart in ML

In this section, we'll delve into real-world applications of Dart in machine learning (ML). While Dart may not be as commonly associated with ML as languages like Python or R, it has its niche and can be a valuable tool for solving practical problems.

1. Mobile App Development with ML

Dart, in combination with Flutter, can be used to develop mobile applications that leverage machine learning models. TensorFlow Lite for Flutter allows developers to integrate pre-trained ML models into their apps for tasks like image recognition, natural language processing, and more.

```
import 'package:flutter/material.dart';

import 'package:tflite/tflite.dart';

void main() async {

WidgetsFlutterBinding.ensureInitialized();

await Tflite.loadModel(

model: 'assets/mobilenet_v1_1.0_224.tflite',
```

```
labels: 'assets/labels.txt',
);
runApp(MyApp());
}
// Implement ML functionality in your Flutter app
```

2. IoT and Edge Devices

Dart can be used on IoT (Internet of Things) and edge devices to perform real-time ML tasks. Whether it's analyzing sensor data, monitoring environmental conditions, or predicting equipment failures, Dart's efficiency and low resource usage make it suitable for edge computing.

```
// Dart code running on an IoT device
void analyzeSensorData(List<double> sensorData) {
// Implement machine learning inference here
}
```

3. Web-Based ML Applications

Dart can also be utilized in web-based ML applications. With the advent of WebAssembly and Dart's support for it, you can run ML models directly in web browsers, enabling client-side ML without relying on external servers.

```
// Dart code compiled to WebAssembly for client-side ML
void predictUsingWebML() {
// Implement ML inference in a web browser
```

```
}
```

4. Custom ML Solutions

Dart allows you to build custom ML solutions tailored to your specific needs. You can create ML pipelines, data preprocessing scripts, and even train models from scratch using Dart's libraries and tools.

```
import 'package:ml_algo/ml_algo.dart';

import 'package:ml_linalg/linalg.dart';

void buildCustomModel() {

final data = [

[1.0, 2.0],

[2.0, 3.0],

[3.0, 4.0],

// ...

];

final labels = [0.0, 1.0, 0.0, // ...

final classifier = LogisticRegressor(

optimizerType: GD(),

numberOfIterations: 1000,

);

final model = classifier.fit(Matrix.fromList(data), labels);
```

```
// Use the custom model for predictions

}
```

5. Integration with Other ML Ecosystems

Dart can serve as a bridge between ML ecosystems. For example, you can use Dart to create scripts that interface with Python-based ML libraries like TensorFlow or scikit-learn, allowing you to leverage the strengths of both ecosystems.

```
// Dart script for interfacing with Python-based ML libraries

import 'package:python_interop/python_interop.dart';

void main() {

final python = Python();

final result = python.eval('2 + 2');

print(result); // Outputs: 4

}
```

In summary, while Dart may not be the most popular language for machine learning, it offers flexibility and the potential for real-world ML applications. Its compatibility with Flutter, IoT, web, and custom solutions makes it a valuable tool for developers looking to integrate machine learning into their projects. With the right libraries and frameworks, Dart can be a versatile addition to your ML toolbox.

Chapter 19: Game Development with Dart

Section 19.1: Introduction to Game Development in Dart

Dart is not only a versatile language for web and mobile app development but also a capable choice for creating games. In this section, we'll introduce you to game development in Dart and explore the fundamentals of building 2D and 3D games.

Why Choose Dart for Game Development?

Dart's suitability for game development arises from its performance, ease of use, and its compatibility with popular game development frameworks. Here's why you might consider Dart for your next game project:

1. **Performance**: Dart's Just-In-Time (JIT) compilation and Ahead-of-Time (AOT) compilation options result in efficient code execution. This is crucial for smooth gameplay and rendering complex graphics.
2. **Flutter Integration**: If you're already familiar with Flutter, you can leverage your existing skills to create cross-platform games using the Flame game engine or other Dart-based game development libraries.
3. **Web and Desktop**: Dart can target both web and desktop platforms, allowing you to reach a broader audience with your games.
4. **Open Source Libraries**: Dart's open-source community has developed various game development libraries and tools, making it easier to create games from scratch or build

on existing projects.

Getting Started with Game Development in Dart

To start game development in Dart, you'll need the following:

1. **Dart SDK**: Ensure you have the Dart SDK installed on your machine. You can download it from the official Dart website.
2. **IDE or Code Editor**: Choose an integrated development environment (IDE) or code editor that supports Dart. Popular choices include Visual Studio Code and IntelliJ IDEA with the Dart plugin.
3. **Game Engine or Library**: Depending on your game's complexity, you can select a game engine or library that suits your needs. Some options include Flame, StageXL, and Three.dart for 3D games.

Creating Your First Dart Game

Let's create a simple "Hello, Dart Game!" example using the Flame game engine. Flame is a popular choice for 2D game development in Dart. Here's a basic structure for your first game:

```
import 'package:flutter/material.dart';

import 'package:flame/flame.dart';

import 'package:flame/game.dart';

void main() async {

WidgetsFlutterBinding.ensureInitialized();

final game = MyGame();
```

```
runApp(game.widget);
// Initialize the game and start it
Flame.images.loadAll(['player.png', 'background.png']);
await Flame.audio.loadAll(['background.mp3']);
game.start();
}
class MyGame extends BaseGame {
// Implement your game logic and rendering here
@override
void render(Canvas canvas) {
// Render game objects and UI elements
}
@override
void update(double t) {
// Update game state
}
}
```

This code sets up a basic game using Flame. It initializes the game, loads assets (images and audio), and defines the game loop for rendering and updating the game state.

In the upcoming sections, we'll explore more advanced game development topics, including game physics, input handling, and creating engaging gameplay. Whether you're a beginner or an experienced developer, Dart provides the tools you need to bring your game ideas to life.

Section 19.2: Game Loops and Rendering Techniques

In game development, the concept of a game loop is fundamental. It's responsible for continuously updating and rendering the game world to create the illusion of motion and interactivity. In this section, we'll dive into game loops and rendering techniques commonly used in Dart game development.

Understanding the Game Loop

A game loop is a core component of any game. It's a continuous cycle that performs three main tasks:

1. **Input Processing**: In this phase, user input is collected and processed. This includes keyboard presses, mouse clicks, and touchscreen gestures. User input is used to control the game's characters and respond to player actions.
2. **Update**: During the update phase, the game's internal state is modified based on user input and game logic. This includes moving characters, detecting collisions, and managing game events.
3. **Render**: The render phase involves drawing the game's current state to the screen. This includes rendering characters, objects, backgrounds, and any other visual elements. Rendering creates the visual representation of the game.

Implementing a Game Loop in Dart

To implement a game loop in Dart, you can use libraries like Flame, which simplifies the process. Here's a basic example of a game loop using Flame:

```
import 'package:flutter/material.dart';

import 'package:flame/flame.dart';

import 'package:flame/game.dart';

void main() async {

WidgetsFlutterBinding.ensureInitialized();

final game = MyGame();

runApp(game.widget);

// Initialize the game and start it

Flame.images.loadAll(['player.png', 'background.png']);

await Flame.audio.loadAll(['background.mp3']);

game.start();

}

class MyGame extends BaseGame {

// Implement your game logic and rendering here

@override

void render(Canvas canvas) {

// Render game objects and UI elements
```

```
}

@override

void update(double t) {

// Update game state

}

}
```

In this example, we've defined a simple game loop using the MyGame class, which extends BaseGame from the Flame library. The render method is responsible for rendering the game world, while the update method updates the game state.

Efficient Rendering Techniques

Efficient rendering is crucial for maintaining a smooth gaming experience. Some techniques to optimize rendering in Dart games include:

- **Sprite Sheets**: Combining multiple images into a single sprite sheet reduces memory usage and improves rendering performance.

- **Culling**: Only rendering objects within the camera's view can significantly reduce the rendering workload.

- **Layering**: Rendering objects in layers allows you to prioritize rendering for better performance.

- **Minimizing Texture Swaps**: Reducing the number of texture swaps during rendering can improve performance.

- **Using Hardware Acceleration**: Leveraging hardware acceleration through Flutter's graphics APIs can boost rendering speed.

In conclusion, mastering game loops and rendering techniques is essential for creating engaging and performant games in Dart. Libraries like Flame simplify the process, enabling you to focus on building exciting gameplay and captivating graphics.

Section 19.3: Physics and Collision Detection

Physics and collision detection are critical aspects of game development, ensuring that game objects interact realistically with each other and their environment. In this section, we'll explore how to incorporate physics and implement collision detection in Dart game development.

Physics Simulations

In game development, physics simulations mimic the real-world behavior of objects. Common physics principles include gravity, friction, velocity, and acceleration. To implement physics in your Dart game, you can use libraries like flame, which provides built-in physics components.

```
import 'package:flutter/material.dart';

import 'package:flame/flame.dart';

import 'package:flame/game.dart';

void main() async {

WidgetsFlutterBinding.ensureInitialized();
```

```
final game = MyGame();
runApp(game.widget);
// Initialize the game and start it
Flame.images.loadAll(['player.png', 'background.png']);
await Flame.audio.loadAll(['background.mp3']);
game.start();
}
class MyGame extends BaseGame {
double playerX = 100.0;
double playerY = 100.0;
double playerSpeed = 200.0; // Pixels per second
@override
void render(Canvas canvas) {
// Render game objects and UI elements
final playerRect = Rect.fromLTWH(playerX, playerY, 32, 32);
canvas.drawRect(playerRect, Paint()..color = Colors.blue);
}
@override
void update(double t) {
// Update game state
```

```
final double dt = t;

// Apply physics: Move the player based on speed and time

playerX += playerSpeed * dt;

}

}
```

In this example, we've added basic physics to the game by moving the player horizontally at a constant speed. You can extend this to include more complex physics interactions like gravity, collision response, and acceleration.

Collision Detection

Collision detection is crucial for determining when game objects intersect with each other. Dart offers various methods for implementing collision detection, including hitboxes, collision shapes, and libraries like flame that provide built-in collision detection.

```
// Inside the update method

void update(double t) {

// Check for collision with another object

if (playerRect.overlaps(enemyRect)) {

// Handle collision, e.g., decrease player health

}

}
```

In the code above, we check if the player's bounding rectangle (playerRect) overlaps with another object's bounding rectangle (enemyRect). When a collision occurs, you can implement custom logic, such as decreasing the player's health or triggering special effects.

In conclusion, physics simulations and collision detection are essential components of game development in Dart. By incorporating these techniques, you can create engaging and realistic gameplay experiences for your players. Libraries like flame can simplify the implementation of physics and collision detection in your Dart games.

Section 19.4: Building 2D and 3D Games

In this section, we'll delve into the exciting world of building 2D and 3D games using Dart. Game development can be both fun and challenging, and Dart provides several libraries and frameworks that make it possible to create captivating gaming experiences.

2D Game Development

Dart, along with the Flutter framework, enables you to create 2D games with ease. The Flutter framework provides a highly customizable and efficient rendering engine, making it well-suited for 2D game development.

Here's a simplified example of how you can start building a basic 2D game in Dart and Flutter:

```
import 'package:flutter/material.dart';

void main() {

runApp(Game());
```

```
}
class Game extends StatelessWidget {
@override
Widget build(BuildContext context) {
return MaterialApp(
home: Scaffold(
appBar: AppBar(title: Text('2D Game')),
body: GameScreen(),
),
);
}
}
class GameScreen extends StatefulWidget {
@override
_GameScreenState createState() => _GameScreenState();
}
class _GameScreenState extends State<GameScreen> {
@override
Widget build(BuildContext context) {
return Center(
```

```
child: Container(
width: 200,
height: 200,
color: Colors.blue,
child: Center(
child: Text(
'Tap to Play!',
style: TextStyle(fontSize: 20, color: Colors.white),
),
),
),
);
}
}
```

In this simple example, we create a Flutter app with a basic 2D game screen. You can extend this by adding game logic, animations, and user interactions to create a fully-fledged 2D game.

3D Game Development

While 2D game development is popular, Dart can also be used for creating 3D games with the help of WebGL-based libraries and engines. One such library is three.dart, a Dart port of the popular Three.js library.

Here's a high-level overview of how you can get started with 3D game development using three.dart:

```
import 'package:flutter/material.dart';

import 'package:three/three.dart' as THREE;

void main() {

runApp(Game());

}

class Game extends StatelessWidget {

@override

Widget build(BuildContext context) {

return MaterialApp(

home: Scaffold(

appBar: AppBar(title: Text('3D Game')),

body: GameScreen(),

),

);

}

}

class GameScreen extends StatefulWidget {

@override

_GameScreenState createState() => _GameScreenState();
```

```
}
class _GameScreenState extends State<GameScreen> {
late THREE.Scene scene;
late THREE.PerspectiveCamera camera;
late THREE.WebGLRenderer renderer;
@override
void initState() {
super.initState();
init();
}
void init() {
// Initialize the 3D scene, camera, and renderer here
// Add 3D objects, lighting, and controls as needed
}
@override
Widget build(BuildContext context) {
return Center(
child: Container(
width: double.infinity,
height: double.infinity,
```

```
child: CustomPaint(
painter: ThreeJSPainter(renderer),
),
),
);
}
}
class ThreeJSPainter extends CustomPainter {
final THREE.WebGLRenderer renderer;
ThreeJSPainter(this.renderer);
@override
void paint(Canvas canvas, Size size) {
// Render the 3D scene onto the canvas here
}
@override
bool shouldRepaint(covariant CustomPainter oldDelegate) {
return false;
}
}
```

In this example, we set up the foundation for a 3D game using the three.dart library. You can extend this by adding 3D models, textures, and interactivity to create immersive 3D gaming experiences.

In conclusion, Dart offers opportunities for both 2D and 3D game development. Whether you're building simple 2D games with Flutter or diving into the world of 3D gaming with libraries like three.dart, Dart provides the tools and flexibility needed to bring your game ideas to life.

Section 19.5: Publishing and Monetizing Dart Games

Publishing and monetizing your Dart games is a significant step toward sharing your creations with a broader audience and potentially earning revenue from your hard work. In this section, we'll explore the various aspects of taking your game from development to distribution, including platforms, app stores, and monetization strategies.

Choosing the Right Platforms

Before you can publish your Dart game, you need to decide which platforms you want to target. Dart offers flexibility in this regard, as you can develop games for various platforms, including:

- **Web:** You can publish your game as a web application, making it accessible to users through web browsers on desktop and mobile devices.

- **Mobile:** If you've developed a mobile game using Flutter, you can target both Android and iOS platforms. Dart's compatibility with Flutter ensures that your game can run seamlessly on both major mobile operating systems.

• **Desktop:** Flutter also allows you to create desktop applications for platforms like Windows, macOS, and Linux. You can distribute your game as a desktop app for users to install and play.

• **Embedded Systems:** If you've developed an IoT game using Dart, you can target specific embedded platforms. This may require adapting your game to run on hardware with limited resources.

Publishing on App Stores

For mobile game developers, publishing on app stores like Google Play Store (for Android) and Apple App Store (for iOS) is a common route to reach a wide audience. To do this:

1. **Prepare Assets:** Ensure that your game assets, including images, icons, and promotional materials, meet the respective app store's requirements.
2. **App Registration:** Register as a developer on the app store(s) you want to target. This involves creating developer accounts, agreeing to terms and conditions, and paying any necessary fees.
3. **App Submission:** Create app listings for your game, providing descriptions, screenshots, and other necessary information. Follow the submission guidelines and policies of the app store(s).
4. **Testing and Review:** Your game will undergo a review process by the app store(s) to ensure it complies with their policies. Address any feedback or issues that arise during this phase.
5. **Publication:** Once approved, your game will be published on the app store(s) and made available for download to

users.

Monetization Strategies

Monetizing your Dart game can take various forms, depending on your goals and the type of game you've created. Here are some common monetization strategies:

- **Paid Downloads:** You can charge users a one-time fee to download and play your game. This approach is straightforward but may limit your potential audience.

- **In-App Purchases (IAPs):** Implement IAPs to offer additional content, virtual items, or features within your game. This allows users to enjoy your game for free initially and spend money on in-game purchases.

- **Ads:** Integrate advertising networks into your game to display ads to users. You can earn revenue based on impressions, clicks, or user interactions with the ads.

- **Subscriptions:** Offer subscription-based access to premium content or features within your game. Subscriptions can provide a recurring revenue stream.

- **Sponsorships and Partnerships:** Seek partnerships with other companies or brands that align with your game's theme. They may sponsor your game or pay for in-game advertising.

- **Crowdfunding:** Use crowdfunding platforms to raise funds for your game's development. In return, offer backers early access, exclusive content, or other incentives.

- **Merchandise and Merchandising:** If your game gains a dedicated fan base, consider selling merchandise related to your game, such as clothing, accessories, or collectibles.

It's essential to choose a monetization strategy that suits your game's genre, target audience, and your long-term goals. Additionally, consider user feedback and adapt your monetization approach over time to optimize both user experience and revenue generation.

In conclusion, Dart provides a versatile environment for game development, and once your game is ready, publishing it and monetizing it are crucial steps. By choosing the right platforms, navigating app store requirements, and implementing effective monetization strategies, you can maximize the reach and profitability of your Dart games.

Chapter 20: The Future of Dart

Section 20.1: Emerging Trends and Technologies

In the ever-evolving landscape of programming languages and technologies, it's crucial to stay informed about emerging trends and technologies that could shape the future of Dart. In this section, we'll explore some of these trends and their potential impact on Dart development.

1. WebAssembly (Wasm) Integration

WebAssembly is a binary instruction format that allows high-performance execution of code on web browsers. Dart's compatibility with WebAssembly opens up new possibilities for web applications. As WebAssembly adoption grows, Dart developers can harness its power to create faster and more efficient web apps.

2. Quantum Computing

Quantum computing represents a paradigm shift in computation. While Dart is primarily focused on traditional computing, it's worth keeping an eye on the developments in quantum computing. Dart could find applications in quantum algorithms and simulations, enabling developers to work on cutting-edge solutions.

3. Dart for AI and Machine Learning

As artificial intelligence (AI) and machine learning (ML) continue to expand their influence, Dart might see increased use in AI and ML projects. Integrations with popular ML libraries and frameworks could make Dart a viable choice for data scientists and AI developers.

4. Extended Platform Support

Dart's adaptability and versatility could lead to further platform expansion. Support for emerging platforms like augmented reality (AR), virtual reality (VR), and mixed reality (MR) may become relevant, allowing Dart developers to create immersive experiences.

5. Enhanced Web Frameworks

Dart has already demonstrated its capabilities in web development through Flutter for the web. Future advancements in web frameworks and libraries could further streamline web app development, making Dart a more competitive choicc in the web development ecosystem.

6. Cross-Platform Development Domination

With Flutter's success in mobile app development, Dart could become a dominant player in cross-platform app development. The continued growth of Flutter's ecosystem and community support will play a vital role in this potential dominance.

7. Improved Tooling and IDE Support

Dart's tooling and IDE support have steadily improved over the years. Future enhancements could further boost developer productivity and make Dart development even more accessible to a wider audience.

8. Community and Collaborations

Dart's open-source nature encourages collaboration and contributions from developers worldwide. The Dart community will likely continue to grow, leading to more libraries, packages, and resources for developers.

In conclusion, Dart's future is bright, with opportunities for growth and innovation. By staying attuned to emerging trends and technologies, Dart developers can position themselves to take full advantage of the language's capabilities and contribute to its ongoing evolution. Whether you're a seasoned Dart developer or just starting your journey with the language, the future holds exciting possibilities for Dart and its community.

Section 20.2: Dart in the World of Quantum Computing

Quantum computing is on the horizon, and its potential to revolutionize computation is both exciting and challenging. While Dart is primarily associated with traditional computing paradigms, it's worth exploring its role in the emerging field of quantum computing.

Quantum Computing Primer

Quantum computing leverages the principles of quantum mechanics to perform calculations that would be practically impossible for classical computers. Quantum bits or qubits can exist in multiple states simultaneously, allowing quantum computers to explore many solutions in parallel. This makes them particularly powerful for certain types of problems, such as cryptography, optimization, and quantum simulations.

Dart's Role in Quantum Computing

At first glance, Dart may seem an unlikely candidate for quantum computing, given its focus on web and app development. However, it's essential to recognize that quantum computing isn't just about developing quantum algorithms; it also involves the broader ecosystem surrounding quantum technologies.

1. **Quantum Algorithm Development**: While Dart may not be the primary language for quantum algorithm development, it can still play a role. Dart developers could work on algorithms that interface with quantum computing libraries and frameworks developed in other languages.
2. **Quantum Visualization and User Interfaces**: Dart's strengths in UI development could be harnessed to create user-friendly interfaces for quantum programming environments. Visualization tools that help developers understand quantum states and operations could become essential.
3. **Quantum Education and Outreach**: Dart's ease of use and accessibility make it a valuable tool for educational purposes. Developers can create educational content, tutorials, and interactive learning platforms to introduce students and developers to the concepts of quantum computing.
4. **Integration with Quantum Development Kits**: Quantum development kits like Qiskit (for IBM's quantum computers) provide APIs for interacting with quantum hardware. Dart could potentially be used to build libraries or SDKs that simplify the integration of quantum computing into Dart applications.

Quantum Computing Libraries and Frameworks

As quantum computing gains traction, libraries and frameworks in various languages are emerging to support quantum development. Dart can leverage these libraries through interlanguage communication techniques. For example, Dart's Foreign Function Interface (FFI) capabilities could be used to interface with quantum libraries written in languages like C or Python.

Preparing for the Quantum Future

While the widespread adoption of quantum computing is still on the horizon, it's never too early to start exploring its possibilities. Dart developers interested in quantum computing should:

- **Stay Informed**: Keep up with developments in quantum computing, including advancements in quantum hardware, algorithms, and software tools.

- **Learn Quantum Concepts**: Gain a basic understanding of quantum mechanics and quantum computing principles to prepare for future developments.

- **Collaborate and Contribute**: Engage with the quantum computing community, attend conferences, and explore opportunities to collaborate on projects at the intersection of Dart and quantum computing.

In conclusion, while Dart may not be at the forefront of quantum computing, it can find its niche in supporting the broader ecosystem. As quantum computing matures, the synergy between Dart's strengths and the demands of the quantum world may lead to innovative solutions and applications that bridge the gap between traditional and quantum computing.

Section 20.3: The Role of Dart in Large-Scale Systems

Dart, originally designed for web and app development, has evolved to be more versatile and capable of handling larger and more complex systems. Large-scale systems come with unique challenges, such as scalability, maintainability, and performance optimization. In this section, we'll explore how Dart can play a significant role in developing and maintaining large-scale software systems.

Scalability and Dart

One of the critical aspects of large-scale systems is scalability—the ability to handle increased loads and growing datasets. Dart can address scalability challenges in various ways:

1. **Isolate Model**: Dart's concurrency model, based on isolates, can help manage scalability. Isolates are lightweight processes that can run concurrently, allowing you to divide the workload efficiently. This enables you to scale your system horizontally by adding more isolates to handle increased demand.
2. **Asynchronous Programming**: Dart's asynchronous programming capabilities, including Futures and Streams, are essential for building scalable systems. They allow you to handle multiple concurrent tasks without blocking the main thread.
3. **Microservices Architecture**: Dart can be used to build microservices, which are an architectural approach to designing large systems as a collection of small, independently deployable services. Each microservice can be written in Dart and communicate over HTTP or other protocols.

Maintainability and Dart

As systems grow in size and complexity, maintaining the codebase becomes increasingly challenging. Dart offers features and practices that support code maintainability:

1. **Strong Typing**: Dart's strong typing system helps catch errors at compile-time rather than runtime. This reduces the likelihood of bugs creeping into the codebase, making it easier to maintain.
2. **Modularity**: Dart allows you to organize your code into modules and libraries. This modularity promotes code reuse and makes it easier to manage and update individual components of the system.
3. **Package Management**: Dart's package management system, pub, simplifies the process of integrating third-party libraries and packages into your project. This helps maintain a clean and organized project structure.
4. **Documentation**: Dart encourages good documentation practices. Well-documented code is crucial for understanding and maintaining large systems, and Dart's tooling supports generating documentation from code comments.

Performance Optimization and Dart

Large-scale systems often require performance optimization to ensure responsiveness and efficiency. Dart provides tools and techniques to address performance challenges:

1. **AOT Compilation**: Dart supports Ahead-of-Time (AOT) compilation, which can significantly improve startup performance. By compiling Dart code to native machine code, you can reduce startup times for your

applications.

2. **Tree Shaking**: Dart's tree-shaking compiler can eliminate unused code during the build process. This reduces the size of the deployed application, improving load times and reducing memory usage.
3. **Profiling and Debugging**: Dart's debugging and profiling tools help identify performance bottlenecks in your code. Profiling tools can pinpoint areas that need optimization, while debugging tools help find and fix performance-related issues.
4. **Concurrency and Parallelism**: Dart provides support for concurrency and parallelism, allowing you to take advantage of multi-core processors. This can lead to significant performance improvements in CPU-bound tasks.

Envisioning the Future

Dart's journey from a web-centric language to a versatile tool for various domains, including large-scale systems, is ongoing. The Dart community continues to innovate, creating libraries, frameworks, and tools that cater to the needs of developers working on ambitious projects.

As Dart evolves, developers should stay engaged with the community, explore emerging trends and best practices, and leverage Dart's strengths to build robust, scalable, and maintainable large-scale systems.

In conclusion, Dart is well-suited for large-scale systems due to its scalability, maintainability, and performance optimization features. Its versatility and evolving ecosystem make it a valuable choice for developers tackling complex projects that demand robust and scalable solutions.

Section 20.4: Dart Community: Contributions and Collaborations

The Dart programming language has seen significant growth and adoption since its inception. A vibrant and active community of developers and organizations has played a crucial role in shaping Dart's ecosystem, contributing to its development, and fostering collaborations. In this section, we'll explore the various ways the Dart community contributes to the language and its future.

Open Source Development

Dart has embraced open source development from the beginning. The language itself, as well as many related projects and libraries, are open source. The Dart SDK (Software Development Kit) is available on GitHub, allowing developers to contribute, report issues, and propose enhancements.

Collaborative Development

Dart's open development process encourages collaboration. Developers from different organizations and backgrounds contribute to Dart's development. Google, as the primary steward of Dart, actively participates in open discussions, reviews, and code contributions. However, Dart's development is not limited to Google; contributors from various companies and the broader community actively shape the language.

Dart SDK and Core Libraries

The Dart SDK, which includes the Dart language, libraries, and tools, benefits from continuous improvements and enhancements driven by community contributions. These contributions range from bug fixes and performance optimizations to new features and support for different platforms.

Package Ecosystem

Dart's package ecosystem has grown substantially over the years. The Dart Package Repository (pub.dev)[8] hosts thousands of packages created by the community. These packages cover a wide range of use cases, from web and mobile development to server-side and command-line applications.

Third-Party Packages

Many third-party packages are maintained by individual developers and organizations outside of Google. These packages extend Dart's capabilities and can be easily integrated into your projects. The open nature of the package ecosystem promotes innovation and collaboration.

Dart Web and Flutter

Dart's presence extends beyond the language itself. Two significant projects, Dart Web and Flutter, have had a substantial impact on web and mobile development.

Dart Web

Dart Web enables developers to build web applications using Dart. It compiles Dart code to efficient JavaScript, allowing developers to write web applications with the productivity and performance advantages of Dart.

---

8. https://pub.dev/

Flutter

Flutter, a UI toolkit for building natively compiled applications for mobile, web, and desktop from a single codebase, has gained widespread popularity. Flutter uses Dart as its primary language, making Dart a go-to choice for cross-platform mobile app development.

Community Support and Education

The Dart community provides support and resources for developers at all levels:

Forums and Communities

Online forums, mailing lists, and social media groups provide a platform for developers to seek help, share knowledge, and discuss best practices. The Dart community is known for its friendliness and willingness to assist fellow developers.

Learning Resources

Numerous tutorials, articles, videos, and books are available for learning Dart and related technologies. These resources cater to beginners and experienced developers alike.

Conclusion

The Dart community's contributions and collaborations have been instrumental in shaping Dart into a versatile and growing language. Its open-source nature, vibrant package ecosystem, and active developer community make Dart an exciting language to work with.

As Dart continues to evolve and expand its reach into various domains, the community's role in its development and support becomes increasingly significant. Developers interested in Dart can engage with the community, contribute to open-source projects, and explore the language's potential in their projects.

In summary, Dart's community-driven development model, along with its strengths in web and mobile development, positions it as a language with a promising future and growing opportunities for developers.

Section 20.5: Envisioning the Next Decade of Dart Development

As we look ahead, it's essential to consider the future of Dart and the potential directions it might take. The programming language landscape is continually evolving, driven by technological advancements and changing developer needs. In this final section, we'll explore some of the possibilities and trends that could shape the next decade of Dart development.

1. Language Evolution

Dart has been on a journey of continuous improvement since its inception. In the coming years, we can expect to see further refinements and enhancements to the language. These may include new language features, improved tooling, and increased interoperability with other languages.

One of the key strengths of Dart is its adaptability. It has proven its worth in web and mobile development, server-side programming, IoT, and more. Dart's future evolution will likely involve accommodating emerging technologies and use cases.

2. Dart for Web Development

Web development is a dynamic field, with constant innovations in web standards and browser capabilities. Dart's role in web development could expand as it embraces these changes. Whether it's optimizing web assembly (Wasm) support, improving web framework integration, or enhancing browser compatibility, Dart will continue to play a part in modern web development.

3. Dart and Flutter

Flutter, powered by Dart, has established itself as a strong player in the world of cross-platform app development. In the next decade, we can anticipate Flutter's growth as it evolves to support additional platforms and use cases. Dart will remain at the core of Flutter's development, ensuring a bright future for Dart in mobile, web, desktop, and embedded applications.

4. Community and Collaboration

The Dart community has been instrumental in shaping the language and its ecosystem. As Dart's popularity grows, community-driven initiatives, open-source contributions, and collaboration with various stakeholders will continue to drive Dart's development forward.

5. Emerging Technologies

The next decade could witness Dart's integration with emerging technologies such as quantum computing, augmented reality (AR), and virtual reality (VR). Dart's versatility and suitability for real-time applications make it a potential candidate for these domains.

6. Education and Adoption

Dart's simplicity and ease of learning have made it an excellent choice for educational purposes. In the coming years, we may see increased adoption of Dart as an introductory programming language in schools and universities, further expanding its developer base.

7. Industry Adoption

As more companies and industries recognize Dart's capabilities, we can expect increased adoption in areas such as finance, healthcare, gaming, and more. Dart's strong performance and reliability make it a compelling choice for mission-critical applications.

In conclusion, Dart has come a long way since its inception, and its journey is far from over. With a thriving community, robust ecosystem, and adaptability to emerging technologies, Dart is poised for an exciting future. The next decade promises further innovation, collaboration, and growth for the Dart programming language. Developers and organizations exploring Dart today are well-positioned to be part of this exciting journey.

www.ingramcontent.com/pod-product-compliance
Lightning Source LLC
Chambersburg PA
CBHW020826261224
19491CB00022B/45

9 798224 866175